PRAISE FOR *PRICING FOR PROFIT*

'This is a stand-out book that helps you not just stand out, but stand out profitably. Best of all, it's such a great read, peppered liberally with so many great case studies. You'll find yourself nodding. You'll find yourself saying "Oh... we can do that!" And perhaps most importantly, you'll find yourself actually doing it too thanks to the way Peter Hill writes this book. It's NEVER a lecture. Rather it's a "come on this journey with me" kind of book. And what a rewarding journey it is. Take it. Do it. Enjoy it. Profit from it.' **Paul Dunn, Chairman, Buy1GIVE1 Pte Ltd and co-author of *The Firm of the Future***

'As a Commercial Banking Director, I have seen many business advisers and attended countless seminars and events, and read many business books purporting to help businesses to improve their profitability but, from my personal perspective, the insight, simplicity and clarity that Peter delivers to his audience is absolutely first class. He gets across complex ideas in simple "real" language that enables readers to understand how they really can apply these ideas in their own businesses. He has a wealth of real-life examples from his own experiences of working with clients, to show exactly how these ideas can be implemented – and the extent to which they do work. In person, he gets everyone in the room completely engaged so, if you ever have the chance to attend one of his seminars, don't miss it!' **David Beaumont, Area Director, Commercial Banking, Devon & Cornwall at Lloyds Banking Group and Non-Executive Director at South West Investment Group**

'If you read this book and think that it is all just good theory, but that it wouldn't work in the real world, you are wrong! Peter Hill worked with my business over a number of years and I can tell you that this stuff really is simple, practical, and it absolutely does work. Adopting and adapting many of the ideas covered by Peter had a profound effect on my business, and uncovered issues that the people within my business were just too close to see. My advice is to buy the book and take the actions suggested, but perhaps most importantly get Peter, or someone like him, to help you drive the changes that are almost impossible to drive from within.' **Stuart Morrison, CEO, Western Electrical Limited**

'There are many ways to improve the profitability of your business but reviewing your pricing has the greatest and fastest impact. And yet most business owners and their advisers ignore it, assuming that in a competitive environment there's little they can do about it. Nothing could be further from the truth. If profit improvement is your goal then this book is the best guide I have come across. Peter Hill has more experience in the field of pricing than anyone else I have come across. In *Pricing for Profit* he presents his findings from many years of helping clients improve their profits. His book is not full of business jargon. Instead, he explains pricing in clear English that is accessible to everyone. This is a "must buy" for all business owners, accountants and business advisers.' **Mike Sturgess, Chairman, SWAT UK, a leading organization that helps accountants comply with regulations, improve efficiency and increase profitability**

Pricing for Profit

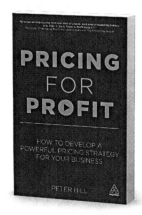

Pricing
for Profit
How to develop
a powerful pricing
strategy for your
business

Peter Hill

KoganPage

LONDON PHILADELPHIA NEW DELHI

First published in Great Britain and the United States in 2013 by Kogan Page Limited

120 Pentonville Road	1518 Walnut Street, Suite 1100	4737/23 Ansari Road
London N1 9JN	Philadelphia PA 19102	Daryaganj
United Kingdom	USA	New Delhi 110002
www.koganpage.com		India

© Peter Hill, 2013

The right of Peter Hill to be identified as the author of this work has been asserted by him in accordance with the Copyright, Designs and Patents Act 1988.

ISBN   978 0 7494 6767 8
E-ISBN   978 0 7494 6768 5

British Library Cataloguing-in-Publication Data

A CIP record for this book is available from the British Library.

Library of Congress Cataloging-in-Publication Data

Hill, Peter, 1964-
  Pricing for profit : how to develop a powerful pricing strategy for your business / Peter Hill.
    pages cm
  ISBN 978-0-7494-6767-8 – ISBN 978-0-7494-6768-5 (e-isbn)   1. Pricing.   I. Title.
  HF5416.5.H55 2013
  658.8'12–dc23
                                                                            2013006912

Typeset by Graphicraft Limited, Hong Kong
Printed and bound in India by Replika Press Pvt Ltd

CONTENTS

ACKNOWLEDGEMENTS

Thank you to my wife Sarah and children Oli, Charlie, Sophie and Georgia who put up with me during the many months it took to write this book.

Thank you also to the many businesses that have placed their trust in me to work with them on the various projects. These have formed the case studies and experiences which are the backbone of the material within the book. Thanks also to Sonja Jefferson, Robert Watson and Liz Gooster who were invaluable in the process of getting it down on paper.

Introduction

Increase your prices – increase your profits. It really is that simple. This book will show you how to do it, and give you the confidence to tackle a subject that is crucial to your business success, so let me be crystal clear. This stuff works. By adopting these simple ideas, every single organization I have worked with has seen dramatic improvements in their business. These range from significant increases in their bottom line profits, to being the difference between survival and failure.

In this introduction, we will consider:

- who should read this book;
- how best to read the book to ensure you get the most from it;
- the relevance of the material to the real world;
- how people don't always focus on the key issues;
- the difference between selling products or services.

Who should read this book

As a guide, this book has been written with the following people in mind: CEOs, finance directors, sales managers, marketing analysts, accountants and strategic planners, and anyone selling directly to customers, in organizations having between 1 and 10,000 employees. The techniques and ideas covered apply in manufacturing, retail, warehousing, transport, professional services, construction, and in every type of *buy stuff – sell stuff* or *buy stuff – make stuff – sell stuff* businesses. It is also increasingly applicable to those government departments, schools, universities, hospitals and not-for-profit organizations that are finding themselves forced into developing more private sector elements to their activities.

Organizations come in all shapes and sizes. There are microbusinesses, often just a single person or husband and wife team running their business from home or a small shop. *Everyone* in this category will learn some great techniques and ideas to help them dramatically improve their approach to pricing and, as a result, their profits. Statistically, over 80 per cent of these businesses fail within their first three years. A focus on pricing would have been enormously beneficial to them, but sadly their business focus was almost always on non-pricing issues.

Then there are many established businesses often referred to as SMEs, or Small- and Medium-sized Enterprises. Whether just a handful of employees or hundreds, these are still predominantly owner-managed businesses with an entrepreneurial leader driving them. Those business owners will get huge value from this book, not only in terms of ideas and techniques they can apply, but also in understanding where the pricing issue gets lost in translation throughout their organization. Additionally, many members of their team such as finance managers or production managers will reap huge rewards from reading the book, and applying the ideas covered. Certainly anyone on the frontline, whether sales manager, shop counter staff or on-the-road salesperson, will get many great tips and techniques to use.

Let's call the final group *Big Business*. You may be the Chief Executive Officer (CEO) of a very large business, or the finance, sales or marketing director for example. This book will help you to see the simplicity of some pricing issues that often become lost when organizations reach a certain scale. This back-to-basics approach to pricing will be a good reminder or it may be a prod in the ribs to get your organization back on track on this all-important issue.

In reality, if you are involved in any area of business and want to improve your skills and develop personally so that you can add value to your organization, then you will benefit enormously from understanding and applying the ideas in this book.

It does not matter what it is that you sell. Although the examples in the book are specific, the concepts and ideas explored apply to all manner of services or to products across a very wide spectrum. You need to read beyond the specifics of the examples and see how the principle(s) can be adapted and adopted by your business.

There is one further category worth mentioning. If you work in a local government or a civil servant role, or perhaps in education or the charity sector, you may find some of the detail frustrating, as it could be much harder for you to implement change within these public sector and not-for-profit organizations. Or if the price of what you do is regulated in some way then clearly your ability to affect change may be limited. The provision of care for the elderly is often funded by local authorities or indirectly by government, and flexibility over price is difficult, but many businesses that feel they have no ability to affect their prices can actually do things in the support areas of their operations. In these businesses you must focus your attention on increasing the value you offer to your end consumers rather than the price you charge.

Increasingly, hospitals, schools, universities and other such organizations are being forced to become more accountable and more independent of government funding, and to become much more commercially aware than ever before. University students now paying high-priced tuition fees are much more demanding on value than they were when that education came free. Applications for degree places fell in the UK when the price appeared to simply treble with no change in what the students received for it. Universities will need to have a much better grasp of the concept of pricing what they offer. Applying the lessons in this book will give anyone in these types of organization a much clearer perspective of an issue that will become increasingly important to them.

How to read this book

The first five chapters cover principles and the basics of pricing, so these offer a valuable refresher for all readers. Chapters 6 to 15 address issues specific to individual areas of pricing, and you may therefore opt to read first the ones that apply directly to you. Overall however, my advice is to start at the beginning and read to the end, because *every* chapter has content that can lead to profit improvements.

Each chapter closes with Action Points. I urge you to stop there, ensure you have absorbed the key messages and *start doing stuff*! Take time to reflect on each chapter before you move on, re-reading it if needed. You will be able to take many of these actions and apply them with immediate benefit, so don't delay implementation until you finish the book. It may well be that several of you in your organization should be reading the book simultaneously, and there will undoubtedly be merit in agreeing how the lessons learned can be applied in your business.

You will get the most from this book if you scribble notes on these Action Points of the things you want to investigate and apply. When people read a book straight through there is always the danger that they get to the end and only remember the points in the chapters most recently read. So pause at each chapter and ensure you have considered how you will take the points and adapt them for you and your business.

Bonus resources

Throughout the book you will find reference to various worksheets and downloadable material to help demonstrate the impact on your profits, and to clarify where you currently are on these key issues. Often you will be asked to gather customer or business information. Some data will be used immediately, and other pieces will become helpful in later chapters. Visit our website at **www.markholt.co.uk** and follow the links or use the QR code shown at the end of the Action points on page 11.

Is it just textbook theory?

The results of getting pricing right are almost instant, always benefi-cial, and sometimes life changing, but the actions needed are nowhere near as complex as people think they are. That's why the word *stuff* is so important. If we use words like *strategies* or *implementation programmes* there is a real danger that some business people will switch off. The simple truth is that the ideas and messages apply just as well to Apple as they do to the corner shop selling apples. That's why I use simple language.

This is not a theoretical book on the economics of supply and demand or the psychology of human decision-making. It is simply intended to get decision-makers in businesses to think a little bit harder about the tremendous opportunity to increase the financial performance of their business by applying various ideas and techniques to their own pricing activities. It does explore some of the basic human reactions and decision-making processes to see how they can help in the 'selling' process and hence the pricing decisions on what to sell at. It is absolutely based on practical reality but please don't make the mistake of thinking that it doesn't have substance or isn't backed up by experience, evidence and facts.

Can you really apply these ideas in your business?

Yes. The ideas explored and techniques used are *real*. They have been used in *real* businesses with *real* customers and *real* problems. They are *practical* ideas that can be applied *immediately* in any business. Your challenge as you work through the book is to identify the ones that apply to you and your business, then to adapt and adopt them appropriately. The biggest challenge is of course to *do them*!

While writing this book, I have drawn from the experiences I have learned working with my own clients (although I have changed their names for obvious reasons), and enhanced this with well-known high street businesses and global companies to make various points. The examples of smaller businesses help to demonstrate the simplicity of some issues, and the others underline the fact that the principles apply whoever you are and whatever you sell. The logic behind all of the ideas will apply to anyone that sells something, whether that is a small one-man plumbing business, or a complex £50m turnover (but still owner-managed) company, or even the likes of Tesco and other huge multinational organizations. So please don't read this book and think *this may work on large business, but not in my small operation*, or vice versa. Read it, and think *how can I use that in my business?*

However, in order to apply the content it is crucial to recognize that everything in business is a moving target. However successful you may be, the world is marching ever forward. Expectations of customer service levels are constantly increasing, technology improves at a faster and faster rate, and legislation, taxation and the general economy are all changing at sometimes alarming speed. Businesses have just not moved forward with their approach to how they set their pricing in the same way. They invest no time thinking about it, devote no resource to the subject, and worry more about relatively minor administration issues than they do about the issue that has the greatest impact on their financial future. It's like wanting better performance from your car and deciding to improve the level of your breakdown insurance. The point is that you will need to keep revisiting the ideas and concepts in the book. There is no single-fix solution.

People don't always focus on the key issues

Some of the issues really are simple, and I often get clients reacting with 'Oh my god, we do that!' or 'Ouch, we make that mistake all the time!' However expressed, the reaction is simply the realization that we often fail to see what is right in front of us.

If you are therefore reading this book and looking for a magic answer, or a piece of software that you can *plug and play*, then you will be disappointed. Although the ideas are simple common sense and sometimes *blindingly obvious*, they all require *action*!

You need to take the idea that applies to you, and do something about it.

Let's start with the first *Ouch*!

Let's look at a typical business seeking to improve profits. How frequently did they address the topic of pricing over the last year? How many hours did they spend reviewing their pricing strategies, researching competitors and adjusting their prices to maximize their bottom line?

Now compare that to the hours they spent discussing whether their salespeople should have an iPad or not. That debate involved every salesperson, every sales manager, every branch manager and the IT team. It took most of the year to resolve, and even covered the internal politics of whether the executives should be issued with one first, whether they needed one or not!

Now think back over the past year of your business. How many hours of effort did your organization put into the critical issue of pricing compared to time spent on issues like the iPad debate? For the bulk of readers, the honest answer will be that pricing is not even on the list of issues to explore.

Ouch!

Whether the decision was ultimately determined by technical aspects, financial restrictions, politics or personal preferences, there would have been many elements to the decision-making process, which all took time. This is understandable, as technology can be expensive, it changes on a frequent basis, and does make a statement about the individual and the organization. It does not matter what your conclusion was, or would be now, it is the process that is the key.

This is not just an issue with technology. Many business owners and managers spend insignificant amounts of time looking at their pricing strategy because they have become swamped by issues such as:

- the details of the annual Christmas party;
- the colour of the boardroom walls;
- the recruitment of the last office junior;
- what car the salesperson should get next;
- the temperature of the air conditioning.

Products or services

This book is about pricing. As such, I often need to refer to what is being sold. This falls into two headings – *products* or *services* – and I have included examples of both to underline key ideas. There is still a danger that if you sell mainly products you could think that an idea only applies to services and vice versa. It is crucial to keep an open mind on how you adopt and adapt an idea irrespective of what is being sold.

If you sell products, these are much more tangible to the customer. They can touch the product and feel it, see the size of the box, the creativity of design on the packaging, and you get the chance sometimes to show the features and benefits of the product on the packaging itself. If relevant you can consider the significance of images, colours and the typeface of the words, all of which can have an impact on the customer's decision to buy. The downside is that customers can see these as isolated purchases rather than part of an ongoing relationship, and be more willing to shop around for comparable items.

If you sell services, these are intangible. Depending on the services you sell, the customer may not even understand what it is you do for them. They know the garage will undertake the car service, but what actually happens in the process is a bit of a mystery. Extend this to services such as providing legal, accounting, tax, or health advice and the gap in understanding becomes even greater.

However, this book is about pricing and how customers' buying decisions are affected by the prices you charge and the way in which that issue alone is addressed and presented to potential and existing buyers. In some areas it explores how the features and benefits of any product or service are expressed, and that can be different depending on whether you are selling a box or an idea.

It is important, though, to just touch on one idea you should consider. If you sell products, these are more often than not regarded as a single purchase decision; eg 'Should we buy that car today?' That places more pressure on a business to make money out of that single transaction, and risks that the customer may never return and present future revenue opportunities.

Conversely, when a business sells services, they have a level of uncertainty that is inherent in the provision of something many customers don't really understand, and that lacks the touch and feel of a nice, simple product. When customers don't fully understand what they will get for their money, or are forced to accept that they cannot change their mind and take something back – the decorator cannot remove and re-roll the wallpaper – the default position is usually to avoid the purchase altogether. Uncertainty causes paralysis and in effect a 'no sale'.

Metro Software Limited (MSL) were at their heart software developers. Their income was from designing bespoke software for individual customers, who didn't really know what they were getting for their money. They also sold *products* such as computer terminals, printers, data storage, etc and provided installation and training. One major change was to get them to *productize* the services that they offered, and to build in additional *services* to some of their products.

Training and support was charged at hourly rates varying between £20 and £50, which caused uncertainty as clients never knew how many hours they would need, or whether the problem was down to them or to a glitch in the software. MSL developed a *product* called the *First Year Training and Support Package*, presented as a box containing a manual on how to use the software, training programmes for users, cards with *what to do when you have a problem* with support-line numbers and self-help guidance. The package was priced at £5,000, based on user numbers, etc. This reduced the potential conflict areas with the client, but also helped to get a much higher price for a clear and simple *product*.

Whenever they sold hardware, they offered a follow-up support programme described as the *Hardware Management Package*. Each follow-up visit helped pick up residual hardware sales and by building in a programme of visits, they added a valuable service to the core product sales and increased the price they could charge as a result.

The message is quite simple. If you sell *services*, try to turn these into tangible products; and if you sell *products*, try to add on services that lock you into an ongoing relationship with the customer. Both will help secure the customer, and increase their perception of value, and hence the price that you can charge.

Summary

If you want your business to be more profitable, look hard at how you price what you do. The impact of even just a few small changes in this critical area on the bottom line is staggering. It is an area that requires much more time and attention than it gets in most businesses.

Every single business that I have worked with on a project to address their pricing has seen dramatic improvements. What you need to do is to invest the time to understand the key issues in this book, consider how you adopt and adapt them to your business, and plan a controlled and sustained approach to implementing change.

This stuff works, you just need to do it!

Action points

1 Look back at your approach to pricing in the last three years and consider the following:

- How often have prices been reviewed?

- How often were prices changed?

- What was the typical change to prices (percentage increases or decreases)?

- What was the cause of each price change? For example, passing on supply cost increases, price-matching competitors, a plan to grow sales volume or profit, etc.

- On the occasions when prices were not increased – but with the benefit of hindsight – to what extent would price increases have had a substantial impact on the profits of your business?

2   Draw up a list of the key people in your team who are currently involved in pricing decisions. Now add to that the names of others who *should* be involved. Consider also whether your whole approach to pricing might benefit by the appointment of a devil's advocate to stir things up a bit.

3   Create a file of intelligence (fact, not anecdotal evidence) on your direct competitors. Assign someone to gather brochures, prices, advertising and any online information about them that includes the value they provide to their customers and the prices they charge. Ensure the pricing team has this data and that it is updated continually.

4   Schedule a workshop with your sales/marketing people and explore where you can *productize* some services and where you can add some *services* to your products.

5   Allocate time in your (others') diaries to ensure regular attention to pricing; ie if you have a monthly or quarterly meeting to work on your business, make sure pricing is on the agenda.

6   Familiarize yourself with the downloadable worksheets and start to gather the financial and other information needed for them. (If you are in a larger organization, you might want to delegate this task.) Visit the website (via the address **www.markholt.co.uk** or the QR code below) and browse the bonus material. This will be really helpful for later chapters and in getting you to see how the issues directly affect your business.

Pricing in context

The objective of every business should be to generate sustainable profit. What you will learn in this and subsequent chapters is that price is the key to achieving this objective and that being the cheapest is rarely a route to profit.

This chapter includes:

- How any business can improve its bottom line.
- The Five Ways to Grow a business.
- A worked example of the impact of each of the Five Ways to Grow.
- Why people fail to see the problem as a price issue.

Business growth will be explored and you will see why price must be top of every business's list of priorities. There are references to downloadable worksheets and material to help you put your own figures into a simple profit calculator and see for yourself the impact of improvements in various key areas.

How any business can improve its bottom line

Improving profitability is not hard. An external perspective helps. Experience of what many other businesses have tried, helps. Diligence to build systems that make employees stick to *best practice* on key areas helps. Motivation to change – based on sharing in success – helps. But what you need is some serious attention to the subject of profit.

So why does it appear to be so difficult to grow profit?

Most business people when pressed to say how they would go about improving profits come up with just two options:

1 Reduce costs.

2 Increase turnover.

Very occasionally they add a third option:

3 Increase productivity.

Although these are right, they are too simplistic as an approach, and they conflict; ie if you want increased turnover you probably need to increase marketing costs or recruit salespeople. If you want reduced costs it may restrict your ability to handle the higher activity levels you hope to have. Often in business the expression *economies of scale* is thrown around as if it was the panacea for all poor financial performance.

> If I can just get the annual turnover up by 10 per cent, my property costs won't change, I will have better buying power, I don't need to add extra people... and with all these economies of scale I will make some serious money!

The truth is it rarely happens. Costs always continue to grow as a business expands, and often growth is achieved by offering customers more for less, so that profit margins fall and the profitability balancing act becomes even tougher.

By using such a blunt approach to profit improvement, owners are overwhelmed by the size of the problem. *Grow turnover* seems simple enough, but *how* is much more complicated.

The Five Ways to Grow a business

All businesses are just a combination of many systems. Systems to buy stuff or make it, and systems to find customers and make sales, as well as all the other systems to manage people and money. The route to improved profit is seen as an improvement in one or more of these areas.

> If only I had a few more customers, or won a few more quotes, or if I could just buy a little cheaper or get my people to work a little harder.

Good businesses will be working on these issues all the time.

When you start a project aimed at increasing profitability, you need to explore the *Five Ways to Grow*. These are:

1 increase the *number of customers* (win more and lose less);

2 increase the *frequency of transactions* (get existing customers buying more often);

3 increase the *average value* of each transaction (higher quality and volume);

4 increase the prices you charge;

5 increase the *efficiency* of the business (people productivity, overhead reduction).

The key to all these steps is to break them down into bite-sized chunks that are easier to understand and easier to address:

- increasing sales is partly about having more customers;

- having more customers is often seen as just winning new ones, but it must also include keeping existing ones;

- keeping existing customers means ensuring that they are not persuaded to switch to competitors;

- stopping customers being poached would require a robust system for proactively contacting them on a more regular basis.

In one professional services firm an approach was implemented whereby A-grade clients would get a face-to-face meeting every month, B-grade only bi-monthly but with a call every month in-between, and C-grades would be seen face to face every three months, with calls and email contacts to bridge the gap. This forced the business to be proactive, and to focus attention on the most important clients.

This is a simple system to minimize the risk that good customers might get stolen by competitors. Most businesses have no such proactive, managed system to force their people to stay in touch with customers (at a frequency that they agree is right). The result is that competitors sneak in, promise to love them more, and steal them from under the business's nose.

A survey of the customers of some large multinational companies sought to categorize the various reasons why some customers had chosen to shop elsewhere. The reasons included:

- *convenience*: another supermarket had opened a new store nearer to them;

- *relationship*: some customers had a relationship with a key individual, and when this person moved on, so did the customer;

- *product/time/price*: they switched because the company couldn't offer the right products, deliver them in the timeframe needed, or were too expensive.

However, the survey found overwhelming evidence that the vast majority of those customers who switched did so as a result of what they described as *perceived indifference*. That is, the customer simply didn't *believe* the company cared enough about them, even if they actually did.

This is the critical point to grasp. *Perceived indifference* was the principal factor in around 68 per cent of all lost business, and *price* was a reason given in less than 10 per cent of cases.

> You will lose around seven times as many customers through perceived indifference than you will through price issues.
>
> Ouch!

Managers need to work on keeping existing customers happy, but they also need to be winning new ones to replace those they lose for reasons beyond their control. Most micro businesses and SMEs:

- don't undertake sustained marketing activity of any kind;

- don't have a simple basic target list of customers (or market segment) to aim at;

- don't have a clear selling proposition and marketing message.

Most operate a low-level, stop-start approach (start marketing when they are quiet and stop when they are busy) with an inconsistent message – Marketing saying one thing, salespeople saying another, and the people delivering the product or service saying something entirely different!

A few very simple processes to ensure consistent and persistent activity can have a profound effect on winning new customers. In a number of even quite large businesses that I have worked with, marketing activity is simply *nil* or involved just sending out branded calendars once each year, when just the simplest low-level, regular and sustained activity can have a huge impact on results.

You should also review the training done by your frontline people in selling skills such as reading body language, listening effectively, and being prepared to handle common objections. Knowing when to go for the close is a critical but often missing sales skill. You need systems to ensure all customers know all the products that you can offer, and are prompted regularly to increase orders and buy extras, etc.

McDonald's are experts in increasing the average value of the sale with the generic 'Would you like a drink with that?' or 'Do you want a Meal Deal?' These are questions that prompt many customers to spend a little more. The vast majority of businesses simply take the order as stated and move on, making no effort to explore up-selling or cross-selling opportunities.

Finally, you should review issues of efficiency (not cost cutting) to see if the business can be made leaner and more effective. This may consider the relationship between people costs and turnover to show where payroll growth is out of tune with turnover either year on year or perhaps branch vs branch. The aim is to ensure that all business costs are value for money and effective investments rather than simply a cost-cutting approach. In fact, in many cases the right answer may well be to spend a little more!

All of the above are simple changes that will improve some aspect of your business. They are the ones that marketing companies, advertising agencies, consultants and others focus their attention on as the route to improved profitability. However, the core subject of this book is, of course, increasing profitability through a clearer understanding of the prices that the business charges.

Below is an example of a typical business turning over £1m. The table shows the base figures for their last financial year and explores the impact of each of the Five Ways to Grow their business.

TABLE 1.1

Example business	Year to 31 March	
Turnover	£1,000,000	
Cost of goods sold	£700,000	
Gross profit	£300,000	30%
Overheads	£250,000	
Profit	£50,000	
Number of live customers at start of year	800	
Number of new customers gained	80	
Acquisition rate	10%	
Number of customers lost	40	
Defection rate	5%	
Number of live customers at end of year	840	
Number of transactions per customer each year	6	
Number of transactions in the year (840 x 6)	5,040	
Average transaction value (£1,000,000 / 5,040)	£198.41	

These numbers are based on a *real* business, and have been rounded for clarity. The table below shows the impact on the bottom line of the five (increasing the number of customers is split into winning more as well as losing fewer) business growth scenarios.

TABLE 1.2

Change	Example action	Impact	Profit increase	Increase from £50,000 start
Acquisition rate moves from 10% to 12%	More marketing	Win just 16 additional customers	£5,710	11%
Defection rate moves from 5% to 3.5%	Improved customer care	Keep an extra 12 customers	£4,282	9%
Number of transactions moves from 6 to 6.1 per customer pa	More pro-activity in sales	84 more transactions at average value	£4,996	10%
Increased average value of sale (more volume or higher quality) from £198.41 to £202.38	Bundle goods into packages	Extra £3.97 on each sale (but with the associated costs)	£5,999	12%
Increased price from £198.41 to £202.38	Simply put prices up	Extra £3.97 on each sale or 2% price increase	£19,995	40%

A small change in winning new customers, losing fewer, or getting a few extra sales or extras on each sale, could all generate roughly a 10 per cent improvement in the bottom line. But a similarly small improvement in price generates a much greater impact on profits and is around four times as beneficial. What's more, all the other areas take much more time, effort and money to implement, whereas pricing is quick and easy to change.

What you can see from the example, and what you will see from your own numbers is exactly what I see *every time* I run the numbers with clients, and *every time* I run a business improvement project with real customers.

That is why this book is focused just on pricing.

> We were really wary of simply putting our prices up, even though Peter explained the numbers brilliantly. But he was right. The change was easy, the customers accepted it without argument, and the impact was immediate and substantial.
>
> MS – CEO Fine Worldwide Goods Limited

Why people fail to see the problem as a price issue

The quickest and greatest impact on profits comes from simply charging a little more on the price. That is both mathematically true, and also the reality in every business I have worked with. Why is it then that when a business seeks to improve profits they almost always pick one of the other Five Ways to Grow first?

Let's consider businesses that send quotes to customers.

What do you think is the single biggest factor affecting whether or not a quote is won?

The reason most businesses don't win a quote for new work is predominantly due to the way in which they manage their whole quoting process. However, the reason most cited by the frontline person responsible is *we were too expensive*. Only when a business considers the whole area can they get key people to agree that it is not always necessary to be the cheapest to win the sale.

No doubt you will have received a quote for double-glazing, or for business services such as accountancy advice. So you know the purpose is to give a price to the customer for them to choose between the alternatives.

Many diverse factors determine whether a quote is successful. The supplier/customer relationship has a big influence as people will often pay a premium where trust is high. Better clarity helps as many customers avoid buying where they aren't sure exactly what they will get. The speed the quote is delivered helps, as a delay creates doubts about the reliability of the supplier to deliver on time.

Most businesses that send quotes:

- don't know their conversion rate (number of wins as a percentage of the number submitted);
- never pursue a quote at all (they simply *wait and see*);
- send a price with no information such as *why choose us* or an explanation of how the price has been calculated;
- never investigate why they were selected, let alone find out why they weren't chosen on the lost jobs.

Finding out why quotes were not accepted and gathering intelligence on competitors gives data to improve future quotes, but the point is that in the absence of these facts or good practices, businesses assume that price is the deciding factor.

What is certain is that the diligence with which quotes are managed has a far greater impact on success than the price. Dropping the price to win more quotes is rarely successful, but having a robust quote management system always is. Get all these things right, and your business will be able to achieve higher prices.

If you think that the way to win more quotes is to be cheaper, you are wrong. Better that you improve your game on how you manage them, so you can command a higher price.

Ouch!

What this specific example underlines is that people in business often do not have the underlying data to know where they can improve their business best to increase profits. The facts are that they lose most of their customers as a result of poor service, not because of price, and they miss out on too many quotes because they didn't chase them hard enough, not because they were the most expensive.

Later chapters offer a wealth of techniques and ideas to help you gather the key data, understand what it tells you and to implement the required changes. Many of the points overlap with others of the Five Ways to Grow. The prime objective is to give you the confidence to charge what you are already worth, as that is the route to higher sustainable profits.

Summary

There are Five Ways to Grow a business.

Of these, getting prices right is the easiest, and it is the quickest way to achieve higher profits. The impact will be greater than any other method.

Most businesses are already worth more than they have the courage to charge.

Action points

1 Work through the Profit Potential worksheet (downloadable at our website **www.markholt.co.uk** or as the iPad app *Pricing for Profit* from iTunes), using the latest annual financial information on your business:

   - Identify the data you cannot easily quantify (ie average defection rate) and ensure you put in place systems to measure them in future.

   - Determine fair estimates for data you cannot easily obtain.

   - Calculate the profit potential from each of the Five Ways to Grow.

2 Consider your current actions to win new business:

- Make a list of any sustained marketing activity that you do.

- Do you have a simple target list of customers (or market segment) to aim at? If not, go and develop one.

- Do you have a clear selling proposition and marketing message that is not focused on how much cheaper you are? If not, develop a simple *reason to buy* message for your target customers.

All this information will be useful later, and if you use your own numbers in some of the examples it will have far greater impact for you.

Worksheets can be downloaded from **www.markholt.co.uk**. Put your numbers into them and see what your profit improvement potential is.

Reader challenge

If increasing your prices right now could yield you a major profit boost (and if you have the authority to do this), go ahead. Send me an email today telling me your intention (as a commitment) and a second email in two months' time telling me what the profit increase was (a fair estimate is OK) – pounds and percentage. I will publish the results anonymously so you can see how you compare to other companies.

Why is pricing so difficult?

Getting to grips with pricing will require you to make some changes in your business, and in any change programme it is important to deal with the objections early. In this chapter we discuss the reasons why most people want to change but don't.

If people aren't open-minded to the benefits of change on any business area, and someone challenges their actions or ideas, then they approach the analysis, research and the detailed debates needed to agree action with their defences up. Rather than hearing it as an honest observation of someone detached from the issue who is just trying to help, they fight the changes with a closed mind.

This chapter includes:

- The importance of knowledge and training.
- How to avoid the impact of your bad experiences.
- Blindly copying the big retailers.
- Limited financial understanding of how profits are made.
- People's desire to please, and their freedom to do so.
- People need to be properly motivated to change.

Many business people have understandable reservations and concerns about changing their business, perhaps thinking *that's easy to say but not so easy to do*! So we need to address the issues that stop owners and managers from pushing the boundaries of pricing, and which may prevent you from using the ideas in this book.

The importance of knowledge and training

How do we get knowledge?

If you want to learn French you would expect to read books, be taught by someone with skills in that area, and practise in some practical way. You would not expect to know it instinctively, nor would you want to simply turn up in France and learn through painful trial and error. Learning the basics of any subject removes the fear of making silly mistakes and gives you the confidence to move forward.

Many people avoid action on pricing because they really don't know anything about the subject. This fear of the unknown leads to indecision and inaction.

What you need to consider for yourself and for your business is what level of skills you currently have on the topic of pricing, what level of expertise you believe you need, and what is the best way for you to close the gap. You are unlikely to have these skills already, so get some training to boost your confidence.

Why are we frightened of pricing issues?

Most people also dislike confrontation, and are careful to avoid situations where it may arise. That's why the majority of people having a really bad meal in a restaurant still answer the waiter's question of 'Is everything OK?' with a 'Yes', even though it's not.

Fear of putting prices up is actually a fear of the unknown, and a fear of confrontation. Consider the conversation between your salesperson and their client when a price rise is being announced. We enter into these discussions afraid of a negative reaction from the customer, such as an argument or them simply saying *no*, and with inadequate preparation for the challenge. The understandable reaction to this fear of conflict is to set and keep prices low.

We avoid raising prices because we are frightened by:

- a fear of the unknown;

- a fear of confrontation;

- a fear of rejection.

Are you too close to the issue?

Now this is far more of an issue in those businesses where the person setting the price is also the person in contact with the customer. Whether the business owner, branch manager or salesperson, those people that can directly affect price (by setting it or by discounting it) and who have personal contact with customers are the most likely to let this fear of rejection cloud their judgement. However, I have seen the same problem with finance directors and CEOs based on either the pressure from below (their own people passing on the fear) or their own personal experiences.

It is a lack of knowledge that causes this fear. If you understood how people made buying decisions, if you properly explored the value you deliver to your customers, if you understood the financial dynamics of your business to know where profits are actually made and what business you should turn away, then you would make completely different decisions. Knowledge in any subject gives us confidence to handle situations where fear may otherwise get the better of us.

Over more than 30 years in business I have met only a handful of people that have received any pricing training, or otherwise invested any time in understanding that key area. Many have indeed read a book or been on a course on sales training, people management, or perhaps even something as routine as how to use Word or Excel, but only a very few on the topic of pricing. It is therefore no surprise that, in the absence of specific knowledge and skills on pricing, most business people take the safest course and avoid the chance of a negative customer reaction by simply keeping prices low.

How to avoid the impact of your bad experiences

Let's add another layer of understandable resistance to change.
Consider the Reader Challenge in the last chapter.

> Why not go back to your businesses today and simply put all your
> prices up 5 per cent and just take the chance that it will work?

Put this book down, save yourself a few hours of time and just jack
your prices up 5 per cent. Don't think about it. Don't try and calculate the impact or pre-judge the reaction, just put them up 5 per cent.

If you are a small business pick a few items and just put the price
up 5 per cent. If you are the CEO of a major business, pick a branch
or whole product line and just force the prices up 5 per cent. Go on,
do it now!

Now, I know that most of you didn't do it before and you won't
do it now. The question is, *why not*?

I know that each one of you right now has the image in your head
of one particular customer who you know would resist any price
increase, or you will have a clear recollection of a past bust-up over
prices. This is not unusual. It is human nature to dwell on the nega-
tives. If you have had bad service in a restaurant and found out they
added someone else's drinks to your bill, you will remember that for
a long time, and probably tell all of your friends.

We remember painful experiences more easily and more vividly
than the nice ones. Most of our actions are driven by two fundamental
desires: pursuit of pleasure or the avoidance of pain. Many studies
have concluded that we work much harder to avoid pain than we do
to pursue pleasure. For example, people will work much harder to
avoid losing £1,000 than they do to earn £1,000.

The problem is that we allow just a handful of painful experiences
on price issues to cloud our judgement on the basic principles.

> We only saw the downside of complaining customers or lost sales, and
> failed to see the upside of higher profits.
>
> DW – Special Events Limited

CASE STUDY

Dr Fun's Amusement Park (DFAP) was a tourist attraction in some financial difficulties, so agreed to increase the prices at the gate by 20 per cent, partially from the need to generate cash and partially because the real value for money was higher than the current prices.

The business became instantly profitable, but, bizarrely, the owner suggested reducing the prices back to the old levels because of the many complaints he was now receiving. On investigation he had around 40 conversations with unhappy visitors about the park and their view of its value for money, some of which were quite heated and upset him. So he wanted to go back to the old prices. A classic *avoiding pain* reaction.

Each complaint could be a family of four, which in context with the 100,000 visitors still meant 99.9 per cent of them didn't complain, but he still wanted to drop the price by £1 for *everyone* purely to avoid conflict with just a handful.

The point is that all of us in business have had at least one painful experience on a pricing issue that is seared into our consciousness. We may have had 100 experiences where customers have been delighted with the value of our services, but it is those negative complaints that stick in the front of our minds.

This is a serious problem for many business owners, salespeople, and the managers, directors and CEOs of organizations, who can overreact to these painful experiences so that decisions on pricing are made with the very worst customers in mind, rather than those who do appreciate and value what we do.

> Always be mindful that your reactions and opinions aren't swayed by the small proportion of customers who have complained in the past or who may complain in the future.

Note: There is more detail on this case study in later chapters and the full case study can be downloaded from **www.markholt.co.uk**.

Blindly copying the big retailers

The problem of a lack of knowledge on pricing is exacerbated by the vast array of pricing messages that are thrown at us and our customers every day.

There is no doubt that many business owners see what big players are up to and copy their actions without understanding the facts or the rationale behind them.

It is common to see discount sales messages (*50% off a sofa!*) in magazines, on TV and on every high street. Some business owners are fooled into thinking that this pricing *strategy* must have been carefully planned to increase sales, and that this generates more profit than the discount that is being offered. Why else would these sophisticated businesses do it?

What they cannot know of course is the cost and hence profit being made on these items. If you are making 80 per cent profit margin, then you can afford to give a 50 per cent discount. Whether you should is another matter. If a business doubled the price they actually wanted to achieve simply to be able to offer it with '50 per cent off', then they are not really giving anything away at all. It is just a selling tool and *not* a pricing strategy.

This issue can be seen in a wide variety of retail pricing ideas adopted by almost all of the major retailers. Consumer magazine *Which?* did a survey of over 700,000 products sold through all the major supermarkets over a year-long study. What they found was incredible and even perhaps questionable as to its legality.

Which? had examples from all of these retailers of bizarre ways that they presented their prices. One example showed ASDA increasing the price of a carton of yoghurt from 30p to 61p, and almost immediately offering a multi-buy deal of 10 for £4. This made it look as though buying a pack of 10 for £4, equating to 40p each, was a saving of 21p or around one-third off the *normal* price, when it was in fact an increase of 33 per cent on the previous price. As soon as the multi-buy offer ceased, the price of each carton was reduced back to 30p.

What this illustrates is that consumers are bombarded by messages promoting price as a reason to buy a particular product, when it is actually only the presentation of the price that is really influencing the customer; ie the volume of yoghurts sold on the 10 for £4 multi-buy deal was much higher than the number sold at even the original 30p price. So it wasn't the price, or more correctly, the value for money that influenced the buying decision, it was the *perception* of great value created by the misleading prices.

Business owners see these pricing messages and feel compelled to compete, or they are under pressure from their customers who have been brainwashed into thinking everything should be discounted, bundled or otherwise reduced in price.

If you intend to use the presentation techniques that these big businesses use, your initial prices must be set at a level to absorb the promotional changes. If you didn't double your prices to start with, can you really afford to offer a 50 per cent off deal? What you need to come to terms with is that these are not *real* prices. You cannot use these price promotion ideas unless you build them into your prices to start with.

There is an upside to this. These businesses have spent lots of money researching the best presentation methods to attract sales, and you can copy these methods easily and quickly. All you need to do is to ensure that your numbers work.

Limited financial understanding of how profits are made

Poor financial understanding is an issue with many small business clients. Sadly, it is also a problem in larger businesses where directors and managers are more departmentalized. It is rare that a sales and marketing director has had any formal training on finance.

If you are confident that you and your key people have a high degree of financial skills then skip this section; if not, take a look at the next few examples and consider how they may be affecting your business.

One of the most common questions accountants get is to explain the difference between *mark-up* and *margin*. I have lost count of how many people have told me they make 50 per cent profit when in fact they only make 33.33 per cent.

Mark-up is the profit expressed as a percentage of the cost price; *margin* is the profit expressed as a percentage of the selling price. The problem comes when the people making the decisions don't completely understand the difference. I have seen businesses mark an item up by 100 per cent – ie doubled the cost to set the selling price – who have then given a 60 per cent discount to placate a customer, believing they could afford to do so. The *mark-up* of 100 per cent is a *margin* of only 50 per cent so they were now selling at a loss.

It would be easy to dismiss this as so obvious that no one would do it. However, if you sell many products with varying cost prices and different profit margins, to a range of customers, each getting different discounts, it is easy to see how busy people can misunderstand the numbers.

I have lost count of the number of occasions that I have found salespeople – acting in good faith – that were offering discounts greater than their profits.

This is almost always a result of a lack of understanding of the numbers, often by those at the point of sale pressured into adapting prices without realizing the impact, but also by those decision-makers setting prices and the discount policy in the first place.

If you look deeper at a business's financial performance, the complexity of the numbers becomes more important. The previously mentioned example of the tourist attraction highlighted the over-reaction of the owner to the complaints of a handful of visitors. What he missed was the simple financial equation that £1 extra from the 99.9 per cent of happy visitors significantly outweighs the consequences of a full refund to the very small number that complained. Ignore the emotional aspect of dealing with this conflict issue and the numbers are obvious.

When business owners are guided towards increasing prices their immediate concern is that they will lose customers. The only important question is *how many*? Will this loss of customers cost more or less than the extra profit they make from the price increase for those that remain?

The sensitivity of sales volumes to price increases varies enormously from product to product and business to business, but calculating how much sales you can afford to lose is just basic maths. For example, a business with a 30 per cent gross profit margin (buy stuff for £70 and sell for £100) could afford to lose 25 per cent of its customers and still make the same profit after increasing its prices by 10 per cent. The point to make is that many businesses simply don't work out these numbers. They are making emotional decisions that avoid conflict.

People's desire to please, and their freedom to do so

In larger businesses there is a huge gap between what the owners believe happens in their business, and what actually happens.

There are many reasons for this disparity, such as a lack of systems to ensure things continue to be done the *right* way. Telling salespeople to chase up quotes is not the same as having a system that monitors the quotes, forces the salespeople to take specific action to follow up, and then reports back to management when it hasn't been done.

However, perhaps the single biggest problem is the desire to please but without consequence. The chapter on discounts covers the problem of frontline people giving away company money by simply 'knocking a bit off' as discounts.

Derrick is a great guy and customers love him. He is experienced and knowledgeable and customers will queue up for him when there are others free to help. They do this for one reason only – he gives them the very best discounts. The more he gives them, the bigger they smile and the more often they come back to see him, so he believes his customers love him. On the whole they do, but only because he gives them the best prices.

The problem is that Derrick is motivated by making customers like him personally, which conflicts with the business's motivation to make a profit. If he hasn't been educated or forced into balancing these issues he will continue to give away the company's money.

Derrick's desire to please people is basic human nature, so we have to put in place systems that force him to be more careful with the discounts or to make him share the pain. This could include getting manager approval for high discounts or having part of his pay linked to the amount he gives away.

Detaching decisions on pricing from those that have direct front-line contact will prevent the two-fold problem that they are overly influenced by a minority of painful experiences, but also prevents them making your customers happy by simply giving away your profit.

People need to be properly motivated to change

The problem is a little deeper than a simple desire to please, and it is linked to the fundamentals of why people do anything at all. Some years ago I worked with a small IT business. There was a problem that the software they designed was bespoke and would inevitably have the occasional glitch. This resulted in irate customers demanding immediate action and being very unhappy when the engineer arrived.

The final idea was that they took a large tin of Quality Street on each visit with the message *munch on these whilst I fix the problem*. Some months later when I spoke with the owner, he told me how well the chocolates were received, that he had won new clients as a result, won extra sales from existing customers, reduced complaints, and that generally it was working brilliantly. His only problem was that apart from him, no one bothered to take the chocolates when they went to clients. I asked him three simple questions:

1 Had he explained to the rest of the staff the impact he believed it had had; ie how many customers had he won, how much new business was gained from existing customers and what the impact was on their satisfaction levels?

2 Was there any penalty for failing to take the chocolates? Did their name go on a *name and shame list* in the staff room? Did three strikes prompt a written warning? Or did he just give anyone a hard time for not doing it?

3 Was there any reward for doing it? Did the person that took the most tins in a month get a bonus? Did the owner publicly say *thank you* and acknowledge the effort? Was there a league table of the *best performers* in the staff room?

It won't surprise you to know that the answer to all three questions was a *no*.

As I explained to the owner, if the employees don't understand the importance of the issue, have no consequence for not doing it, or no reward for doing it, you don't need to be a genius to know that it isn't going to happen.

The same principle applies to the issues of pricing. If we expect employees to understand without training, and to adopt a new practice without encouragement and reward for success, or challenge and penalty for failure, then they will simply fall back to the actions that give them personally the least pain or the most pleasure. What we need to do is to link their actions directly to their own pleasure (bonus scheme) or pain (warnings and embarrassment), so that they don't give the business's money away with impunity any more.

The desire to please is a very strong one. If employees are given freedom to make customers smile by simply giving them your money, then in all likelihood that is exactly what they will do. You need structure, rules and control, and reward when they do it right. Even business owners can be drawn into keeping customers happy through knocking the price down without thinking through the consequences of this short-term or knee-jerk reaction to a challenge on the price.

Summary

Raising prices may upset many people in your organization, so you need to invest time and effort into re-training people in order that their energies can be re-directed away from resisting the changes and towards achieving higher profits

It is crucial for any business that wants to improve its profitability that it has a clear understanding of the hurdles it needs to overcome to achieve this. That may be further financial training or simply more consideration of the most common mistakes made in pricing.

In most businesses a project to attack the issue of pricing will require some significant change. As such the people it affects must understand what changes are needed and why, and that there are consequences to fighting or ignoring the changes as well as benefits and rewards for embracing it.

Action points

1 Think carefully about your attitude to business, your motivation to improve and whether your experiences may blinker your willingness to explore ideas and make changes.

   - Complete the worksheet Explore Your Attitude to Pricing (downloadable at our website **www.markholt.co.uk**).

   - Identify the Derricks in your organization, and put in place authorization levels for the discounts they (and others) are allowed to give.

   - Identify a list of those people within your organization who directly affect the prices you charge; mark those that require training on pricing issues.

2 Find a local trainer who can help train your team on the key issues. These may vary wherever your business is based, but try:

   - your local Chamber of Commerce and Industry;

   - your accountant;

   - the RAN ONE organization;

   - your bank manager.

3 Download the Pricing for Profit iPad App from the App Store and explore where your business can have the greatest impact on profits. I guarantee that price will be top of the list.

The remarkable benefits of getting pricing right

We have explored the profit improvement potential through smarter pricing in context with all of the other ways to improve your business, and looked at the principal reasons why people struggle with the whole issue and so fail to maximize their profit.

This chapter covers four brief case studies that underline some of the difficulties of implementing change generally and on the issue of pricing specifically. Visit our website at **www.markholt.co.uk** and follow the links to download the full case studies.

This chapter covers:

- Understanding what you actually charge at the moment.
- Increasing the headline price (but with added value).
- How you can charge more when you guarantee value.
- Making sure your frontline people understand the profit equation.

Understanding what you actually charge at the moment

CASE STUDY

Fine Worldwide Goods Limited (FWG) was a £1.5m turnover business providing security services to a wide range of clients. It was doing OK, delivering profits and surviving well within its regional marketplace. The three owner/directors of this business were concerned that the business was not maintaining its marketplace position and that it was under increasing pressure to deliver more and more for its customers while charging less and less for doing so.

They started a year-long project to review their business and implement a series of changes that would enable them to regain their market position and also improve the underlying profitability. Countless issues were uncovered, and a wide variety of tools were used to research the key points, develop initiatives to handle them, and then train the team members in the changes proposed. Perhaps the most enlightening was the mystery shopper exercise.

When the owners met with the frontline salespeople and discussed some of the ideas, they were met with a wall of objections based around what competitors were apparently up to: 'How can we charge that price if X Limited is charging less, or we can't charge a callout fee, as our main competitor doesn't?' These were normal concerns that are encountered in any similar project, but, as usual, based purely on anecdotal evidence and assumptions of what the other businesses were up to.

Try as they might to argue the points, the wall of objections remained. So they undertook a mystery shopper exercise using an external adviser. The adviser agreed with them who their main seven competitors were, and then contacted these businesses and asked them to meet him at his offices to pitch for the opportunity to take him on as a customer. To get a good comparison he also got one of FWG's team (who did not know of his role) to pitch as well.

It was an illuminating experience for these business people. One of the eight salespeople turned up was a little worse for drink, but at least he turned up, which is more than two of them did! Several launched into exactly what they could do for the adviser without having asked him any questions about what he wanted or needed from them, and only two put forward a sound pitch and a clear proposal for working together. One was FWG and the other their major competitor.

This exercise gathered a huge amount of valuable information about all the other businesses. They knew their competitors' account opening procedures.

They had copies of their marketing materials and a good idea of their selling approach and the key points they always made. Most importantly they had a very clear understanding of their competitors' prices and the different packaging options that they were offering.

When the adviser analysed this information with FWG's directors and sales team, they were astounded by what it showed. This is, of course, often the case with mystery shopper exercises, as it is perhaps understandable that in the absence of facts people simply assume that competitors are better and cheaper than they are, and they build up these reasonable concerns into unfounded fears. Just like walking into a dark scary house, people are frightened of all the things they imagine might be hiding under the bed or behind the door, until they turn on the lights and see that these fears are simply in their heads.

What the business found in this case was that they were not the most expensive, and they actually delivered better value for money than all but one of their competition. As a result, they spent time analysing all the data, essentially taking the best ideas of the competitors to improve the marketing messages, beef up the sales pitch, and re-structure the various packaged deals into more compelling offers. What the business gained was the confidence to really believe that they were worth the prices they were now prepared to charge because they knew exactly the service, quality delivered and prices charged by their competitors.

A side effect of this analysis was a detailed review of each individual product cost and their selling prices to see what gross profit they made on every item. On more than a quarter of their products they actually sold the item for less than it cost them to provide it.

The business was able to identify the items where the actual price charged (after the discounts given to customers) was less than the cost, how much below cost it was, and how many of those items they sold in the last year. Had they simply sold these products at cost, then the business would have made £100k more profit during that year!

The action taken was to review the price of every single item being sold below cost and adjust those upwards by increasing prices and limiting discounts.

Once again, there were a number of factors that affected the overall results, but raising the prices was the most significant. Over the course of the next nine months the business was able to see the volumes of each item sold and to quantify what revenues they would have achieved at the old prices and compare this with the sales figures actually achieved. The result was that they were now generating profit at the rate of £11k per month more than they did previously, such that in the next full year this would equate to over £130k of additional profits. This was 8 per cent of their turnover, but had the impact of trebling their bottom line.

- Get the financial facts now.

- Identify all products that you sell at a loss.

- Fear of competitors can only be overcome by getting the facts.

- Get frontline people on board with changes, and challenge any negative reactions.

Increasing the headline price (but with added value)

In Chapter 1 we considered the Five Ways to Grow your business. These were:

- increase the *number of customers* (win more and lose less);

- increase the *frequency of transactions* (get existing customers buying more often);

- increase the *average value* of each transaction (higher quality, volume and price);

- increase the *efficiency* of the business (people productivity, overhead reduction).

CASE STUDY

In Chapter 2 we looked at a brief case study of Dr Fun's Amusement Park (DFAP). I was introduced to the family who owned and ran this business by a friend that had concerns about their situation. I knew the park well having visited it with my own family, but I was not aware of the precarious financial situation that unfolded from that initial meeting

Like many family-run businesses, it had started as a hobby that had just grown over the years. They started with a single 'ride on' steam train, and became a substantial tourist attraction with 100,000 visitors a year. The problem was that it had rarely been profitable in the preceding 20 years, and had survived only by borrowing against rising property values.

As a result, they had not been forced to address their weak financial performance and poor business management skills. This is a real problem for many organizations where owners, CEOs, directors and managers don't address weaknesses in their businesses until the point at which they have no choice – by which time it can often be too late. In DFAP's case, recession meant that asset values had fallen and as a result so had the bank's security, and faced with continuing losses and an increasing debt, the bank issued the ultimatum of 'get the business profitable within the current year or we will close it down at the end of the season'.

There were a number of elements to the situation that you may recognize. First, the business had never been properly managed. All key roles were occupied by family members, none of whom had any great skill in running a business. They relied instead on their knowledge of the business from living and breathing it for over 20 years.

Another important factor was that they were right at the edge of the precipice. The bank had issued their ultimatum, and was beginning to take control. Repossession of the business and the loss of incomes for all of the family was a very real threat, so that they had little choice than to get serious about changing. In this project and with others in similar situations, decision-makers tend to accept the guidance given to them much more readily when the business is in trouble. Often, incredible amounts of time are wasted persuading owners to act on what are simple and obvious points, but without the external pressure of a bank demanding action it is often hard to get them to make those changes.

> It is imperative that any business monitors performance and acts early when these start going wrong.

Fortunately we had time. Our meeting took place in late February, so that we had an Easter Holiday period within a month and the whole of the summer holiday to make the changes count. Being a predominantly cash business, the impact of changes was felt almost immediately in the bank position. Compare this to, say, a building company where the time lag between action and result could be 3, 6 or even 12 months, and the advantage of working with a cash business is obvious.

The only real negative was the fact that the initial assessment had identified a great many weaknesses; so there was such a lot to do that we could well overload the family with the work needed. Usually, a gradual decline in profits is a result of a number of areas that require attention. The problem is that many business people will attack areas they feel most comfortable with, such as customer service or marketing, when pricing is the one that will have the greatest and quickest impact on the bottom line.

What the example below illustrates is what is possible with a planned and well-managed project that deliberately seeks to improve the *profit* of the business. Many people miss this key point and focus on improving *turnover* in the hope that it leads to increased profits. It is also fair to say that there were some parts of the project that were not related to how they priced the entry fees, food, drinks and souvenirs. For example, they uncovered – and stopped – significant theft of cash from the business, which is not the subject matter of this book. However, irrespective of these issues the overwhelming impact on profits was from the pricing changes implemented.

The entry price of the attraction was £5.95 per adult, with a number of variations for children, babies, OAPs, family tickets and groups. The proposal was to increase the entry price by 20 per cent. This was a big jump, but it was based on detailed market research on competitors, as well as customer surveys on what visitors liked and why they came in the first place.

Although the family were right behind the idea of boosting profits, it still took a great deal of persuasion before they were happy to put up the prices. Their acceptance came when we suggested offering something else to justify the uplift in price with an increase in value. So we developed the idea of a *free return*. Visitors who paid full price would be able to visit *free of charge* as many times as they wanted over the following seven days.

There were concerns about monitoring the return visits, but our research confirmed two key things. First, that only an insignificant number of visitors were already returning, preferring to try other attractions or use the beaches or other free facilities, rather than pay again to visit somewhere they had already experienced. This was important to ensure we were not giving away income by letting existing customers who currently paid to return, back in for free. Second, that the average spend per head was quite low as many visitors brought picnics and their own drinks to keep their holiday costs down.

Once the free return was operating, we were able to prove that 21 per cent of visitors came back for at least one additional visit. Further research found that these returning visitors were often going to the beach until it got too cold and then *popping in* to DFAP for an hour or two in the late afternoon, or going shopping in the local towns and then heading to the attraction when the kids had had enough retail therapy and wanted to let off some steam. Previously, visitors would simply not have come for a half-day visit when it cost the full price entry, but they now did so because it was a *free return* visit.

The most important point was that while these visitors were getting additional visits for free, the average spend per head showed a huge increase. On the free visits customers spent money on food, ice creams, drinks and souvenirs because they hadn't had to spend cash on getting into the park. The average spend went from £8.20 per head to £10.40 per head. The fact that it took two or more visits to achieve this didn't matter.

So what was the overall impact?

The business turned over £1m a year. It was losing money and had done so for many years. The year's accounts that reflected the period over which the project was run, showed profits of £150k on similar visitor numbers. Perhaps the most important issue was that the bank did not call in their loans, and allowed the family to trade on and restructure their business and eventually to recover financially.

That example was one of the most dramatic improvements in such a short space of time, with just 10 weeks of analysis and hard work implementing the changes before the start of the summer season. After this we simply monitored all the numbers through the busiest part of the peak season to ensure the changes were continued, and to react if necessary to any negative impact.

- Customers are the only people that can really determine the value of what you do.
- You need to get facts on what competitors charge.
- Find out why customers don't come back, by doing market research.
- Seek to add value at the same time as a price rise.

How you can charge more when you guarantee value

CASE STUDY

Another tourism-related business, Coastline Vistas Limited (CVL), owned and let holiday homes. The business had been stable for some years, but struggled to make a decent profit simply because of the costs of running the business. They could have run 100 homes with the same infrastructure and personnel and would then have made a good profit, but they only had 40 homes and hence it was hard to massively increase revenues as a route to increasing profits. These properties seemed to be worth more than the owners currently had the confidence to charge. Indeed you could have rented one of their luxury four-bed homes with state-of-the-art TVs and fully fitted kitchens, etc for the same price as a caravan on a holiday park.

A price increase of £100 per week on each one was suggested. This was based on research of comparable accommodation in the same area. The client was understandably concerned as the nature of holiday rentals means that if you set prices too high or too low, then you are stuck with these for the whole season. Too high and you get no lettings; too low and you are busy fools for four months with no profit at the end.

What I suggested was that we add the £100 to the price of each week's holiday, but with a special *Summer Sun Guarantee*. The offer was: *If it rains for more than half your holiday, then you will get £100 cash back to contribute towards the cost of indoor activities, since you would be unable to enjoy the countryside or the beaches for free.*

There was an incredible amount of debate about rain-monitoring systems and when refunds would be triggered, but that was immaterial. If it rained, they were only giving back this additional £100 that they would not have otherwise had. No competitors offered this guarantee.

The purpose of the exercise was to test the customers' reaction to the higher prices, in order that the client might gain the confidence to hold or even increase these prices in the next and subsequent years. It was all about testing the market and exploring how presentation of pricing affects buying decisions.

The running costs of the business were unaffected by the price change. It is possible that they lost a few customers where the headline price now appeared too high, and with people who didn't see value in the guarantee; but it is equally possible that they gained a few who loved the idea, which many told us.

The only important question is whether they made any more money as a result. In that year the turnover increased by £50k from letting the properties at an extra £100 per week over the summer. From this we then needed to deduct the amounts given back under guarantee. So how much did we give back? Nothing at all. Fortunately, the weather was great, and no one asked for refunds. The business made £50k more profit, doubling what it would have made without this price change.

You may be reading this thinking that it has no relationship to your own business either in scale or in the industry you work in. The point is much simpler than that. The fresh perspective on their business, looking at it as a profit-making machine, considered a number of ideas to improve the results. Despite resistance to the changes, this course of action more than doubled the results of the previous year. Could they, or would they, have come up with this idea on their own, and would they have had the courage to try it without external pressure? No. When you read on through the book, I guarantee that there will be other simple ideas and actions you could take that may well have the same impact on your business, but if you only see the reasons not to have a go, then you won't make a penny more.

- Put prices up but have a safety net to catch any customers that object.
- Find clever ways of presenting a price increase.
- Work out how many customers you can lose for a given price increase.

Making sure your frontline people understand the profit equation

CASE STUDY

Special Events Limited (SE Limited) was a huge multi-branch company with £20m annual turnover and healthy profits, achieving outstanding improvements by focussing on pricing.

They agreed to run a series of courses for all of the frontline people who were in one way or another involved in setting prices for customers. This included branch managers and department heads involved in setting list prices, and many others who set prices through the back door by giving various levels of discounts to customers at the point of sale.

It was important to raise the awareness of all of those frontline people to the consequences of their actions. The training sessions uncovered some incredible pricing inconsistencies between branches and even between individuals within the same branch. A key part of the project was to gain consistency in pricing and discounting practices across the whole company.

When we started, the business was making a gross profit margin of 22 per cent, across all of its products; ie on average for every £78 it spent on goods for sale, it achieved a selling price of £100. By the time we had finished, the business was making an average margin of 27 per cent. Turnover in that period had continued to creep forward, and we monitored the enquiries-to-sales ratios to be satisfied that we were not losing loads of sales as a result of holding our nerve on prices and giving away less in discounts. The increased margins equated to broadly a 6 per cent price increase, so it could easily have had a negative impact if poorly managed.

So, what was the impact on the bottom line?

The gross profit margin went up from 22 per cent to 27 per cent. Taking out the general turnover increase, this meant that the gross profit value on the core £20m sales increased from £4.4m to £5.4m in the year, an increase of £1m. There were some costs of handling the issue, not least of which was taking 130 people out of the business to participate in training sessions to understand and implement the various changes. There were some quite significant changes to their bespoke computer software to monitor who gave discounts to whom and why, so that they could maintain the changes agreed. In reality all these costs were significantly less than £200k leaving around £800k of real retained bottom line improvement. So although the business was already achieving around £2m a year of pre-tax profits, adding another £800k or 40 per cent improvement was a fantastic result.

This extra profit quickly became extra cash as debts were collected, enabling the business to finance its continued expansion and investment in technology and new equipment.

- Quantify how much margin is lost to uncontrolled discounts.

- Training frontline people on pricing issues is critical to successful implementation.

- Get consistency across each branch and each individual with how prices and discounts are applied.

What you can see from these examples, and those in later chapters, and what you would see in every single one of the specific projects to improve profits, is that it is actually quite straightforward to make simple changes that can have a huge impact on the bottom line.

Whether motivated by financial difficulties or by a desire to make more money for future investment and growth, or even because the owners/shareholders want the kind of return on effort and risk that they deserve, doesn't matter. The analysis and actions are the same. These wider business-improvement projects often cover a large number of different aspects, such as customer service issues, marketing activity and customer-relationship management as well as the profit-critical issue of pricing. Every business can increase prices by simply adopting a better approach to the way it charges and any improvements in these other areas can only help support a firmer line on pricing issues.

As detached advisers we can quickly identify underselling issues; ie where the business lacks the confidence to charge what it is already really worth, and lacks sophistication in the way that it does so. Even if this seems obvious to us as external advisers, we cannot always get the business's decision-makers, whether one-man-band owners of small- and medium-sized businesses, or the CEOs, directors and managers of much larger organizations, to accept the points. As a result they don't accept the need to increase prices and to add some smarter thinking to the way these are presented to customers.

So we need to consider other points such as customer services standards, product quality, reputation and market position, the competition, the quality of its sales and marketing activities and a whole host of other issues demonstrating the value that is being undercharged for at the moment.

There is a double-whammy effect in that many of these key business areas are revisited by the decision-makers for the first time in years. Time, effort and debate are applied to how they can be improved, and the understanding of their impact on bottom line profit is raised. It may be that this self-analysis actually helps raise their game in the key areas that enable them to charge more, or it may be that they gain a clearer understanding of what they already do and how this compares to others. The overall objective is to help the business to have the confidence and the underlying quality to charge prices that enable it to make a decent profit.

A key point is that hardly any businesses invest any significant time in analysing *how* they can improve profits. Whether faced with an urgent need to improve their financial performance, or simply a desire to make more money, almost all of them approach the problem of profit improvement generically by seeking to increase sales volumes and/or reduce costs.

What these projects do is to challenge the thinking of the owners and decision-makers who are blinkered by their internal perspective and limited to knowledge of their business or of their industry. It is crucial therefore that you retain an open mind as you read the detailed content of this book, or, if possible, work with someone outside of your business to help you to challenge your own ideas or established practices. That could be your accountant, or even another business owner you know for whom you can reciprocate.

Every single project we have run has seen an increase in bottom line profits, and the bulk of these improvements have been derived from changes in the prices they charge and the way they manage and control this issue.

Don't be in any doubt that you can improve your profits, and that pricing is the first place that you should start.

Summary

This stuff works. The examples above are just a few to illustrate how quickly and how easily profits can be increased with just a little more attention and perhaps a little more sophistication to the subject of pricing. You may well be able to double your profits with a clearer focus on your pricing strategy.

In every one of these examples the decision-makers had reasonable concerns about the reaction of customers and the resistance from employees, but all proved unfounded. The impact was dramatic in every project, and in many cases has been the difference between survival and failure.

Action points

1 Do an analysis of your profits and identify areas where profits and losses are being made. To what extent do you have under-performing branches that are being subsidized by others, or some product lines or customers that are losing you money?

2 Identify your top 5 or 10 major competitors, and do a mystery shopper exercise.

   - Gather financial information on their businesses, see what margins they achieve, and what bottom line results they deliver.

   - What one thing do they do better than you, and where are you better?

   - Based on these ideas, develop three things that you can do to improve your offer to customers.

3 Download and read the full case studies and identify all of the specific actions that you could apply to your business, and develop a plan to adopt and adapt the appropriate ones.

4 Implement that plan.

04 How most businesses price and why these methods are wrong

Having worked with hundreds of businesses and business owners over the years, the mechanics of how most prices are set can be boiled down to just four main methods. We need to explore each of these so that we understand them, and to explain the weaknesses in each method. Having done this we then consider the only critical element of pricing, which is to better understand the value your customers place on what you do.

This chapter considers four principal pricing strategies, and then the only one that really works:

- Cost plus pricing – the fundamental flaw.
- Undercutting competitors – it simply cuts your profits.
- Last year's pricing plus a bit – the bit is never enough.
- Best guess pricing – it's just a stab in the dark.

And most importantly:

- Value to each customer – the only pricing strategy that really works.

Cost plus pricing – the fundamental flaw

The flaw in cost plus pricing

> The most common method of setting prices is to take cost price and to add a set percentage mark-up. This does *not* work.

Cost plus means adding, say, 30 per cent, 50 per cent or even 100 per cent to the cost price of what a business buys or makes to set the price at which they sell. There are many complex ways of doing this, but they all have the same flaw.

CASE STUDY   Smithfield Clothing

Mr Smithfield ran a small business that sold outdoor clothing. At a meeting he complained that he had been extremely busy over the weekend, and when I asked him why, he told me the following:

> For many years he bought stock from a key supplier. His volume of sales had grown so that he was now buying much more from them, so he decided re-negotiate the cost of all his purchases, based on these higher volumes. He was delighted to say that he had managed to negotiate a 15 per cent discount off all of his current purchases.

This was a great result, but didn't explain why he had been so busy. He continued to explain his pricing method:

> He took the cost of each individual item he sold and doubled this to set the selling price. For example, an item that cost £10 would be priced at £20 giving a gross profit of £10 and a profit margin of 50 per cent.

> Having been successful in negotiating a buying discount, the cost price of all of his stock had reduced by 15 per cent. For example, the item costing £10 now only cost £8.50 and hence was sold at £17. He therefore explained that he needed to re-price all of the items that he purchased from that supplier. That was why he had been so busy.

The mathematics makes sense to me, but the logic of this pricing method is completely flawed. So I worked through the example he had used to show him that where he used to make £10 profit, he now only makes £8.50 – although it remains a 50 per cent profit margin, the same item now generates £1.50 less profit than it did a week before. It is pretty simple when you think about it. He had passed on all of the discounts he had negotiated because his buying price and selling price were directly linked, so as his buying price fell, so did the profits.

While this example stems from those with a rigid formula with selling prices linked to cost, it happens more frequently where businesses have established what they regard as *normal* profit margins. Another business – Wholesale Equipment Supplies Limited (WES) – had a buying team focussed on negotiating better buying prices from all of the suppliers that they used. However, the company had established what they regarded as *normal* profit margins on everything it sold. Every time they negotiated a discount on the buying price the front-line salespeople gave it all away to the customer by increasing the discount on the selling price. (Chapter 10 covers this point.) So although they did not have the rigid formulaic approach adopted by Mr Smithfield, they informally adopted the policy of a *normal* profit margin, and ended up with the same problem.

It really is quite simple. If the customers valued the item at £20 last week, that does not change based on a lower cost price to you! If Mr Smithfield's customers were happy to buy the pair of waterproof trousers for £20 that is because they believed that the trousers were worth that much. The fact that the cost had reduced by 15 per cent had no impact on their perception of this value, not least because the customer didn't even know what the cost price was before.

Interestingly, what often proves this point to businesses is to consider the opposite situation. Just consider for a second what most business owners would do if their cost prices suddenly went up 15 per cent.

When another company, SE Limited, were unfortunate enough to have a price increase of 10 per cent imposed on them by a major supplier, it was greeted with a moan from all the frontline people saying, 'We can't possibly pass that on to our customers, they would all leave'. Many times that argument was accepted and some of the price increases were absorbed by the company, at least in the short term. So if the logic of a link between buying and selling price doesn't work when cost prices go up, then why would it work when they go down?

The vast majority of businesses I have met would probably take a similar view that they couldn't pass on all of an increase of that size straight away. They have therefore accepted that the value to the customer and the cost to them are unconnected issues, yet when cost prices reduce they often feel obliged to reduce their selling prices and sometimes, like Mr Smithfield, or SE Limited, they *deliberately* reduce them.

Later chapters look at the setting of prices without connection to cost, based solely on the value to the customer, and there are a number of techniques for managing the internal reaction of any frontline people.

> Businesses that use any formula to link buying price to selling price often end up accidentally passing on all the discounts they have gained to their customer, thereby reducing their own profits.
>
> Ouch!

Undercutting competitors – it simply cuts your profits

Many businesses deliberately set their prices at a level they think is just below that of their main competitors. They do this in the expectation that this will attract new sales from those competitors or win sales where customers are choosing between them.

There are a number of issues with this, some of which are dealt with in other chapters. However, the fundamental problem with this strategy is that there is always someone else around the corner prepared to do what you do for less money. The ability to be the cheapest and still make a profit is really a preserve of organizations with incredible scale and who sell such huge volumes that the elusive *economies of scale* are a reality. This would include the likes of Tesco, and ASDA/Walmart. This is a perfectly legitimate business strategy, but it is simply impossible for the small owner-managed business or even those with tens of millions in turnover to achieve. However, I just want to focus on the accuracy of the data to support the argument that undercutting competitors is a viable plan.

It is crucial to engage the frontline people in generating ideas to support price increases. However, there is often a barrier where they complain, 'We can't put our prices up as our customers will just buy from competitor XYZ who are cheaper'. They then underline this by saying how their customers often make that very point during negotiations.

My simple challenge is to ask, 'How do you know what XYZ are charging?' Their answer in most cases is that their customers tell them.

What we find is that the decisions on price are made almost entirely on *anecdotal* evidence. What's worse is that the hearsay is biased as the customers clearly have a vested interest in persuading us to keep prices low.

It is critical to gather the facts on what prices are actually being charged by the business's main competitors. This is pretty easy, you can do it with a few simple phone calls, online research, or even a mystery-shopper programme to actually go and buy a range of core products. I have seen this done in businesses to identify pricing inconsistencies across various branches, and to prove to the business owners and managers that what they think is happening within their business is not what is actually happening at the sharp end dealing with customers. In every single case the *estimates* or *expectations* of the business based on their informal customer feedback are way out of line with the actual prices that their competitors are charging. In short, the assumptions and the facts don't tally. The other advantage of such a research programme is that it yields information on competitors' marketing activities, account opening procedures, selling propositions and standards of service, all of which help to establish the comparable value delivered by each business.

Like many issues within this book, a key part of the problems businesses encounter is because they make decisions based on flawed information, whether biased, anecdotal or simply inaccurate.

> Setting prices to undercut your competitors makes no comparison of the difference in the value delivered by them and by you, and secondly, it is more often than not simply based on incorrect anecdotal evidence. Get facts or lose profits.
>
> Ouch!

Last year's pricing plus a bit – the bit is never enough

The next most common pricing approach is to take *last year's pricing plus a bit* as a simple pricing model. Almost always this *bit* is the underlying rate of inflation, but it can be any arbitrary small percentage uplift. Sadly, it can also in reality be last year's pricing *less* a bit, but after reading this book that should not happen in future!

The problem is the same as with the cost plus approach – the price charged is not linked with the value to the customer.

If you increase your selling price based on, say, the increase in all prices that form the country's inflation rate, it assumes that there is value inflation in the marketplace; ie just because inflation runs at 3 per cent, does a customer feels the item is worth 3 per cent more to them a year on?

The inflation rate includes price increases that are to a great extent not *optional* increases such as energy costs, food, etc and it therefore doesn't reflect an increase in the average customer's recognition of value. This is even truer when price inflation is running ahead of wage inflation. Consumers are less willing to simply accept that prices go up by inflation if that isn't reflected in their pay packet.

CASE STUDY Bright Sparks Limited

A large electrical contractor business had a policy of increasing prices once a year based on the underlying inflation rate. This was for many years a 3 per cent to 5 per cent uplift, and it was broadly accepted by customers.

However, over a short period, two things happened. First, a large element of their cost is the installation of electrical cables in various sizes and grades. A high-cost element of these cables is copper, which saw a surge based on a worldwide shortage of the material. Consequently, while inflation overall was running at around 3 per cent, the price of their largest raw material jumped over 10 per cent in a single year. Their annual inflationary increase just didn't keep up with underlying costs, and rapidly ate into their profits.

Bizarrely, they had the opposite impact over another two-year period, where wages experienced a freeze in the market based on high unemployment and pressure on jobs, while underlying inflation continued at around 4 per cent. When the company tried to add on the usual inflationary uplift, many of their customers wouldn't accept it based on the freeze in wage costs.

Inflation is perhaps the most common component of a last year's pricing plus a bit approach, but it is simply not linked to the financial realities of any business in the short term. It only works if customers' appreciation of what you offer inflates in the same way. Recent economic difficulties have clearly shown that value inflation doesn't exist, as many businesses have not been able to raise prices at all despite an underlying increase in their own costs shown by the inflation rate.

In some markets, there is even value *deflation* as increased competition or improved technology drive overall prices down. The cost of making a digital camera model ABC1 may not change much when model ABC2 and ABC3 are launched, but its value in the market will almost certainly fall if these newer models have higher megapixels, faster shutter speeds or simply extra features that the old one doesn't. Adding a small percentage to reflect inflation ignores the fact that your actual costs may have gone up well ahead of inflation, meaning that profitability will still fall.

A customer's appreciation of value doesn't change just because inflation means that your costs do. So don't expect to be able to pass on your higher costs without increasing the value you offer.

Ouch!

Even if you had done a great deal of thinking and research when you originally set your prices, when you adopt a last year's pricing plus a bit approach these prices will very rapidly detach from the value the customer sees and thus become nonsense.

Best guess pricing – it's just a stab in the dark

By this term I don't mean randomly plucking figures out of thin air, rather a decision based on what price to charge that doesn't link itself to cost price, to what competitors charge, or to whatever was charged the previous year, and certainly not based on proper market research or financial analysis. It is simply based on *judgement, instinct* or to perhaps be more accurate, an *educated guess*!

Many professional firms, such as lawyers, have now been forced into fixed price agreements rather than the traditional rate per hour. They need to look at the work required, estimate how many hours this will take and what level of team member the work will require, and then calculate a fixed price for the customer. By necessity this will require a judgement based on experience. Similarly, a plumber may use his experience to set a price at say £500 for a boiler repair job. The issue is that although these appear to be based on a calculation of the work needed, they eventually are simply an educated guess based on historical experience.

Many will have set pricing for a job, which is the same for all customers in all circumstances, hoping that they are right more often than they are wrong.

The key point is that these prices are not set based on a carefully thought through decision-making process to establish the *right* price or the *market price*, just a finger in the air based on experience of the market. This is absolutely not *value pricing*, described below.

CASE STUDY   The Friendly Lawyers partnership

Working with one law firm, all the lawyers were asked to provide an estimate of the fees they would charge based on a clear brief of the client's problem. This was, for example, a debt dispute for lawyers in the commercial team and a divorce for lawyers in the family team.

Although the paperwork was standard, the range of potential fees indicated was staggering. The highest figure was roughly double the lowest on most areas we looked at. This showed a huge inconsistency between individuals and across departments. They may all start with the same broad view of the work involved, the same rates per hour for the individuals needed on the task, but depending on many other factors the proposed price varied greatly. This is due to factors such as each lawyer's current workload and hence keenness to win the job, their personal experience of delivering that particular service, and whether they think they are in a competitive tender situation. There may simply be a confidence variance between individuals, with some naturally more bullish on fees than others.

Slight variations are understandable, but leaving lawyers to individually set prices showed variations between £5k and £10k for the same work. One solution was to set guide prices for all services, and to insist on peer review before doing any quote. This improved consistency and enabled partners to talk each other up or down as appropriate.

You cannot simply set prices based on experience and judgement as this is fundamentally flawed by the human element. Personal experiences and individual characteristics, such as confidence, overshadow the importance of research and facts.

Ouch!

So how should businesses set their prices?

Value to each customer – the only pricing strategy that really works

In a perfect world you would set a unique price for every single customer based on the value to them of each individual product or service you provide, and at that specific point in time. That is value pricing.

This would take into account factors such as their ability to pay, so you might charge more to those customers who can afford it and less to those who can't. Now that is not just the fact that they have the money to pay, but actually that our perception of value is distorted by our financial situation. I would never think flying first class was value for money when I have to work as hard as I do to pay for it, but if I won the lottery and had £5m in the bank, I may well decide to fly first class. The product hasn't changed, the value on offer is the same, but my perspective on it has changed. So should the supplier charge more just because I can pay more? We might also consider the significance of the item itself at that point in time, so that if a customer is desperate and needed your product right then, the price could be higher than if they had time to shop around.

There are many readers who will struggle with these ideas. They would see it as profiteering or perhaps ripping people off. You can make up your own mind as you read through the rest of the book. You may want to consider, though, that every business should make a profit which reflects the effort and risk that they take each day that they open for business, and very few achieve this. This may mean that the business will need to seize opportunities to make very good profits on some transactions, and accept lower profits and perhaps even losses on other transactions, knowing that it will balance out over time.

The reality is, of course, that it is very difficult to have unique pricing for each customer, and therefore we end up having a more generic approach. Eventually this evolves into a one-size-fits-all pricing policy, where all customers pay broadly the same irrespective of circumstances. The problem with this is the same as we might have if we operated a one-size-fits-all clothing policy. In clothing we would need to have the largest size possible in order that everyone can at least wear it, however ridiculous it might look on smaller people. With pricing this simplicity of one-size-fits-all means that the prices are driven down towards the lowest prices that appease the most price-sensitive customers, and are way below the levels the top customers could and would pay.

The overall critical objective is to set prices based on the value to the customer. Consider a new model smartphone for example. The cost to make this is around £120. If the manufacturer adopted a cost plus mentality they might double it or even treble it. If they adopted a last year's pricing plus a bit approach, they might take the previous model price and add say 20 per cent for the uplift to the newer one. The manufacturer of course wants to get the best price possible and they do a lot of research to establish what the perception of value is within its marketplace. How does it compare to the alternative products customers could choose? Are typical customers spending business money or their own cash? Even down to some specific market research that would ask: 'How much would you pay for a phone that did this?'.

Based on the information Apple gathered, they set the price at £500. This captures the early adopters that buy it because they must have the latest model, or the geeks that want the most up-to-date technology. As demand reduces, or newer versions are brought to the market, they will gradually reduce the price to sweep up more customers for whom the value perception may be lower. They absolutely never rely on just anecdotal evidence of what their competitors offer and at what price. They will know every detail of the alternative products, having researched them extensively in deciding where their own products sit within that very crowded marketplace.

Imagine a young man who ventures into a car showroom. In front of him is a shiny red convertible sports car. He wanders around it looking at all the gadgets opening the doors, putting the roof up and down, and examining all of the buttons and knobs. The salesperson offers him a test drive where he hears the roar of the engine, and feels the exhilaration of speed.

He gets back to the showroom and the salesperson launches into the sales patter covering all the features and benefits, optional extras and eventually the price and the easy-payment terms that are available.

Now, he will of course need to consider lots of issues before he can make a buying decision, such as whether he can afford to buy or to run the car. He will need to consider whether it is a practical option; ie whether he has kids or a dog to transport. He may also need to consider how it will be perceived by others; ie does it provide the image that he aspires to, and depending on his circumstances, whether his wife or girlfriend would approve!

Think back to the last time that you bought a car, and the wide range of issues that you considered, particularly for what is of course one of the most expensive purchases that any of us buy in our lives. You may have decided that the satnav upgrade wasn't worth the price, but that the leather seats option was. What were all the questions you asked the salesperson when selecting the model and specification of the car you chose?

What I am certain of is that neither the young man looking at the red sports car, or you when you bought your last car, sat down with the salesperson and asked, 'Can you tell me how much it cost the manufacturer to make it?'

There is a really simple point here.

The way in which you set prices requires a degree of thought and research that very few businesses invest in. How can you set prices that maximize the profit your business makes without research, analysis, testing and then training to react properly to the responses from customers?

For each of the options it is important to think about what you would do if circumstances changed, as in the cost plus example. If your cost price went up 25 per cent would you expect to pass this on, and could you? What if it fell by 25 per cent, would you drop your prices to match?

What if you aimed to be just under your competitors' prices? If they dropped them by 25 per cent would you do the same? Could you? If they increased them, would you?

> The customer decides the value of what you do. What you pay for an item, what competitors charge, or what you charged last year has no real impact on this figure.
>
> Ouch!

Summary

The only true way to set your selling prices is through value pricing, which is establishing a value to each of your products for each of your customers and then pricing them accordingly.

What I see time and again are businesses that operate a pricing policy which is far too simplistic (to make it easy for them to calculate) and linked to some formula that ignores completely the value to the customer. To make matters worse, when the costs or competitors' prices change, most businesses lack the courage to move their prices up when needed, yet almost always drop the prices in a blink when their costs or competitors' prices fall. If you want your prices and profits to increase, you will need to tackle these issues.

As with most things in business, it is all about value for money. The cost price, what competitors charge or even economic factors such as inflation or interest rates may influence pricing decisions, but the value to the customer is the only real issue.

Action points

1 Consider how well researched your prices are.

   – What methodology did you adopt in your last three price changes? Are there any examples where you have value priced?

   – Where you have followed competitors' actions, how well researched was your data?

- If you have used any of the four wrong ways to price, have your pricing team remove the option to follow these and to develop your own value-based proposition.

2 Plan out how you can gather research that will help you understand your options:

- Identify your top five competitors.

- Do some simple online or telephone research on a sample of products or services where you compete.

- Undertake a full mystery-shopper exercise.

- Pick some of your core products and track your buying and selling prices over the last five years. Look at the trends and set up a workshop to debate when and how the next price changes should be handled.

- Lock in Price Review dates for the next three years.

Understanding value versus cost

There is a simple principle that underpins many of the ideas used in pricing. In order for a sale to take place, the buyer and the seller have to agree on the right price for the product or service. This may sound obvious, but there are a surprising number of situations where they don't agree yet a sale still takes place.

What you will see in this chapter is that the only important element in pricing is the value to each customer.

This chapter includes:

- The Value Scales.
- What happens when the scales don't balance?
- How to balance the scales.
- The dissipation of value over time.
- The importance of discussing value with customers.

The previous chapter looked at the most common methods of setting price and concluded that value in the eye of the customer is the only real issue. This chapter considers the issue of value in more depth.

The Value Scales

The seller will set their price taking into account a range of issues that they consider important, such as the raw cost of whatever product or service they are selling, the delivery costs, the business running costs and the profit they want to make. It is rarely that well thought through, but clearly there is an objective of selling at a price that does at least generate an apparent profit.

The buyer does a similar assessment of alternative suppliers and alternative products, and essentially determines whether the value to them of acquiring the product or service is equal to or greater than the price they are being asked to pay. Now this may happen at a very basic or even subconscious level, but an assessment of some kind is made.

Let's translate this idea to a set of scales. On one side is the price that the supplier is seeking to charge in order to get what they want from the deal. Let's say this is £100, so initially the scales would be tipped completely towards *No Sale*.

FIGURE 5.1

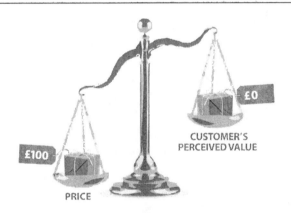

£0

CUSTOMER'S
PERCEIVED VALUE

£100

PRICE

NO SALE

On the other side of the scales is the *perceived value* to the customer; ie the amount that the customer is happy to pay based on what the product or service is worth to them. If that figure was also £100, then that would be seen as a *fair deal* and the sale may well happen.

FIGURE 5.2

PRICE   CUSTOMER'S
              PERCEIVED VALUE

FAIR DEAL

If the customer's perception of value was as high as £120, then they would see it as a bargain, and a sale is even more likely to take place.

FIGURE 5.3

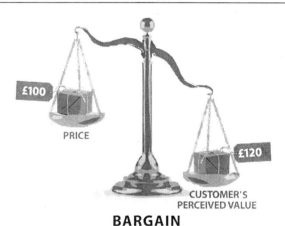

PRICE

CUSTOMER'S
PERCEIVED VALUE

BARGAIN

In both these situations it is still possible that the buyer may question the price as an automatic reaction. Your salespeople therefore need to be wary of thinking that such a challenge is a genuine concern about *value*.

However, let's assume that the customer's perception of value is actually only £80.

FIGURE 5.4

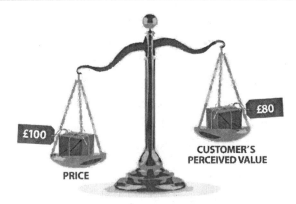

NO SALE

If this were the case the Value Scales don't tip far enough towards a sale taking place. The buyer simply thinks that the product isn't worth the price, so no sale would take place.

What happens when the scales don't balance?

The most common outcome is for the supplier to simply discount the price by £20 to the £80 that the customer is happy to pay. This is done far too often, and far too quickly. The problem is that this discount falls straight to the bottom line profit, and can crucify the profitability of many businesses that fail to understand this key point. (Chapter 10 covers the whole area of discounting in great depth and considers why this happens and a number of options that can be discussed as an alternative.)

The second point is that the customer may temporarily accept paying the extra £20 and *over-pay* for the goods or services. This may sound ridiculous; why would someone pay more than they perceive something is worth? It may be that they just don't have time to shop around or argue the price in this instance, or that they are very happy indeed with other products and services from the same supplier and that this individual item is simply not important enough to worry about. In many cases this dissatisfaction only materializes *after* the event when they reflect on the deal or when alternative suppliers offer their deals. On many purchases there is a post-transaction period of doubt where customers worry they have bought the wrong thing or paid too much.

The problem with this solution is that the customer has not changed their perception of the *value to them*. It is just that in this instance or on these products, they are prepared to tolerate what they see as over-pricing. However, the reality is that this will linger as dissatisfaction.

Acceptance of the price does not mean that they are actually happy with it.

Customers may passively shop around for the next purchase or the issue will fester between supplier and customer. What is clear is that eventually a customer regularly paying more than they perceive something is worth will become unhappy and leave.

How to balance the scales

The best option by far is an open exploration of each side's respective perception of value to see where the differences lie. If, for example, the supplier perceives that giving the customer extended credit is highly valuable, but the customer does not, then they may agree a reduced price for cash payment with order. If the supplier feels that same-day delivery is a key feature but the client does not, then they may agree a lower price if the buyer collects. Quite often it is simply that a customer does not appreciate the features and benefits that are included within the deal, such as free delivery, guarantees and extended warranties, immediate availability, etc.

I didn't appreciate all of the features and benefits of buying from the company because the salesman never mentioned any of them.

Charlie Oliver

It is only by discussing all of these issues that the differences between each side's perceptions of value can be understood. Sometimes the scales can be made to balance by simply raising the customer's appreciation of features and benefits to the level the supplier wants to charge. It may be that the supplier is able to identify some features that the customer doesn't value and remove these from the deal before reducing the price.

So what are the two critical issues on the Value Scales?

The biggest issue is that these differences are rarely explored in any depth. The most common reaction to any difference of opinion on values is for the supplier to simply reduce the price. This is done as a result of the poor selling skills of the person at the frontline and poor training and systems to deal with this very common problem. In later chapters you will learn some techniques that allow you to work with customers to review the price issues properly.

Just one simple model that works really well is the price triangle, illustrated below.

FIGURE 5.5

When the customer challenges the price of, say, fitting a new kitchen, the salesperson will respond by saying something like:

Yes of course we can negotiate on the price. Let's just look at the options.

They will then draw the triangle and say:

> Which two of these issues is most important to you?
>
> Our prices are set to enable us to do the quality of job that our customers want, within a reasonable timescale. I can only reduce the price by taking longer, say by using fewer people, or fitting your job in around others. Or I can reduce the price by reducing the quality of the materials or workmanship.
>
> In other words, I can do it cheap and I can do it quick, but it will not be as good. Or I can do a good job and I can do it cheap, but it won't be quick, or alternatively I can do a good job, I can do it quick, but I cannot also do it cheap. So what aspects are most important to you?

The logic of this is pretty obvious to most customers; ie if you want great quality and great service, then this must come at a price. What most customers want to aim for is a place somewhere in the middle of the triangle where the product or service is delivered to a reasonable standard, within a reasonable timeframe and at a fair price.

The message is simple. If price is the only issue that you discuss, then it will only be price on which they make their decision. If you want customers to agree with your view of the value you place on what you do, then you must explore it with them and ensure they understand all of the features and benefits you deliver.

The next point is that it is the customer's *perception* of value that determines the price that they are prepared to pay. That perception can only be based on the features and benefits that they know about, hence the point above that these must be explored as part of the sales process. Many businesses offer a fantastic range of features and benefits, but neglect to mention these. They may be unique features of the product or service, or just aspects of the way the business operates. But if the customer doesn't know them, they cannot place a value on them. Consider the box below and whether you offer these features and whether you explicitly discuss these with the customers at the point of the sale.

Examples of typical hidden features of a sale:

- Offering credit terms (pay over 12 months or after 30 days).
- Specific product guarantees (14-day return policy).
- Specific service guarantees (providing a loan item during repair period).
- Warranties (replace broken parts with 12 months).
- Training (showing the customer how to get the best from the product or service).
- Installation (trained engineers will set up the product).
- Delivery (held in stock for next-day delivery, or cheaper if collecting).
- Instant availability (reducing waiting time to zero for crucial products).
- Technical knowledge and experience (can offer advice on the right purchases).
- Exceptional customer service (friendly people and free tea and coffee, etc).
- 24-hour call out (no problems from a delay in repairs).

There are many more features that different businesses can offer depending on the products or services they sell. There are thousands of obvious and common features and some quite unique and exceptional features. The key is that if the business simply assumes that the customers know these things, even where they may be existing long-term customers, they will be wrong. It is essential to believe that customers know none of these features and benefits and to ensure they are automatically included in any sales dialogue. If not, how can the business expect its customer to place a value on them?

We have always had a 24-hour call-out service, with phone diverts and rotas to handle it, but we then realized that the salespeople never mentioned this to any of our customers. When we challenged them their response was that they didn't want to get calls in the middle of the night!

David Victor, Mechanical Support Services Limited

The Value Scales need all of these issues to be covered if the supplier is to avoid the damaging option of simply reducing the price.

But the critical point is that it is the customer's perception that determines the value, not the actual cost of that component.

CASE STUDY

One project uncovered an example where a customer went into a business to see if they could supply a particular product. The salesperson checked, confirmed that they had the item in stock and that it was £500. The customer argued that this was more expensive than other potential suppliers, and the salesperson agreed to discount the price by 20 per cent to £400.

A director of the business was watching this exchange, and asked if he could have a few moments with the customer to ask a few questions. Did he know, for example, that the business offered a trade account and therefore 30-days' credit? The customer said this was of no value to him because he always paid cash on the day.

Did the customer appreciate that the business had technical experts that could talk with him about whether that product was the best answer, or whether a newer product may be a better solution? The customer explained that the item was specified on a customer's job and they had no ability to use alternative products.

Did the customer know that the business offered same-day delivery of items if ordered by lunchtime, to reduce the time he spent visiting his suppliers? He did like this, but said in this case he needed the item that afternoon and would not have placed the order by the requisite time.

The final question was the most critical:

Did the customer appreciate that the company held £2m of stock so that customers could be confident that whatever they wanted, it was almost certainly in stock. Yes, he explained, this was very valuable to him, as he had already visited five other suppliers and been unable to source the product he needed anywhere else!

Now, do you think the salesperson would have been so ready to give the £100 discount had he known he was number six on the list of people to try, and that the only reason the customer had used them was that they were the only ones that had the item in stock. Probably not!

This is a blunt example, but the message is very important. If you do not consider all of the elements of the deal that sit on your side of the Value Scales, then it is impossible for the customer to place any value on these features and benefits themselves. If you genuinely believe an item is worth £100, then you need to ensure your customers know why you believe this by getting the salesperson to discuss all the elements of the deal. If you still don't agree and the scales still don't balance, you can look to take items out of the deal or add new ones in, rather than just dropping the price to match the customer's perception.

The issue of value was covered within the previous chapter with the example of Mr Smithfield. In this illustration he linked his selling price of a product to its buying price. When his buying price fell, so did his selling price. However, the customer's appreciation of value did not change, not least because customers didn't even know what the buying price was.

The dissipation of value over time

Consider another aspect of value to further illustrate the point.

A man is charged with a very serious crime, and seeks out the best barrister he can find: 'Get me off this charge and I will pay whatever you ask.'

The day of trial comes and he repeats his promise to pay *whatever it takes*.

At the end of the trial he is acquitted and thanks the barrister, reminding him to send his bill as whatever it is he will pay it immediately because it was worth every penny. He was really worried about being convicted and couldn't have done it without the barrister's expertise.

The busy barrister takes a month to raise the invoice for his fees at £20,000.

When the man receives the bill he is astounded by its size remarking that it was an open and shut case, and that he was clearly innocent, and that all the barrister had to do was just to turn up.

What this demonstrates is that the value of the product or service changes over time. If the barrister had said up front that it could cost between £20,000 and £30,000 the man would in all probability have written a cheque there and then if asked. By leaving the issue of price until after the event, the appreciation of value has dissipated.

If you have ever had financial difficulties, a tax investigation, or even a positive business opportunity, you will have wanted the issue tackled as a priority because speed and quality are more important to you than the cost at that point in time. The value of the solution at the beginning of the task is much greater than after it is finished.

The importance of discussing value with customers

What is perhaps more important is that the value to the customer may be higher than the supplier thinks it is. So many times a sales-person who has been asked for a price will simply leap in with a figure.

Let's consider a plumber who has been asked for a price to install a new heating and hot water system. He puts forward his price of £5,000.

The customer then says: 'Brilliant, I thought it would be twice that much.'

Of course, as soon as he has put this figure on the table it is very hard to move it up. By failing to uncover the issues with the customer in advance and ask some pertinent questions he has missed a big opportunity. He could have said:

> A new heating system could cost between £5,000 and £10,000
> depending on some options for you to consider. For example, a standard
> boiler costs around £3,000, but if there are a number of people in the
> house using showers or running baths at the same time, you may want
> a more powerful option. Equally, there are some slightly more expensive
> boilers that are much more energy efficient in the long term and more
> reliable. The other consideration is how long the job will take. I can opt

to have three men on the job so that it is done as quickly as possible with the least disruption for you, or I can make it slightly cheaper by having one man on the job, but it will take a lot longer. What are your preferences?

As you can see, some of this is, in effect, simply a better sales approach, and a slight variation on the *Good, Quick, Cheap* triangle above, but the key element is to establish a price range and to explore with the customer where they are in terms of affordability and the value of the key options to them. If a customer does want the best job, as quickly as possible, they will be drawn to the top end of the price range based completely on the *value* to them of the various elements. More often than not there will be a reaction of either 'I was only expecting £3,000 to £4,000, can you work to that?' or 'That's fine I was expecting it to be around £10,000'. Any reaction is OK, as the objective is to get some indication of their price expectation.

Summary

Knowing your costs and being able to configure pricing that enables you to make a profit is an essential business skill. However, this must be accompanied by a very clear understanding of what value you are offering, presented in terms that the customer can easily digest.

You must avoid an overly simplistic price structure based on the cost to you of delivering your product or service, or at the very best based on what you *think* the customers' perception of value may be. You need mechanisms to explore the value to each customer in order to set a price that works for you and the customer.

Don't be afraid to state the value you are giving, and always offer a higher value option at an increased pricing level. The way to get the price up is to ensure that customers understand all of the components of value, and they will only understand them if you tell them.

Action points

Set up a team to include key people in your staff (include people from sales, finance, production and anyone dealing directly with customers). Get this team to:

1 Compile a list of your major products/services. You will revisit this many times, so begin with a list of your top 20 most profitable items.

2 Run a workshop for a small group of senior people from sales, and production. Ask them to record all of the value features and value benefits of the top 20 items, from the perspective of the customers.

3 Ask the team to brainstorm ways of offering extra value to the top 20 items. Get them to set a Premium level of pricing to those items. Involve a finance person in this area of the work.

4 Using that information, have your sales or marketing people amend the brochures and web pages that customers see, and also train the sales force to present the values to customers. This includes conveying to existing customers exactly what the value is in the existing products/services they buy, and an introduction to the Premium offering.

5 Set up a programme to roll out to customers, explaining the existing values of each top 20 item and the new Premium offering.

6 Ask your finance people to monitor the profits coming from the top 20.

Packaging for higher prices

When most businesses set their prices, they do so assuming that customers will generally buy only one of a single product each time. They don't even set these prices with any great sophistication and generally assume a single purchase for each sale.

However, they do understand that there is a high cost and a great deal of effort required to achieve each sale. All of the firm's marketing and brand promotion, and a lot of its infrastructure has been created in the broad hope of generating sales and therefore a small part of all these costs is applicable to every sale.

A part of growing a business is to increase the value of each sale, and pricing can be a key tool in achieving that goal.

This chapter includes:

- The four ways to maximize each sale.
- Using price to up-sell and cross-sell.
- Offering choices increases the value of the sale.
- Alternative price options affect the perception of value of all options.
- Setting price differentials properly.
- The price of pain.

The four ways to maximize each sale

It makes sense to most business owners and managers that they should seek to exploit the opportunity and maximize the sale at that point.

There are four ways to achieve this:

1 By selling a *greater volume* of the items than the customer intended to buy; ie they asked for three reams of copy paper and the salesperson persuaded them to buy a box of five.

2 By selling them *complementary products* at the same time. When a customer buys a book on Amazon, there is always a panel with other ideas under the heading *Customers that bought this product also bought these...* . In a large number of businesses this will be seen as the sale of one core product, together with the various consumable items or additional features of the service. As consumers we see this situation when we buy a TV or fridge and are offered the five-year extended warranty option.

3 By persuading the customer to buy a *higher specification* product that has a higher price. This could be as simple as a more expensive wine from the menu in a restaurant, or it could be upgrading to business class. Car dealers advertise their cars at the entry-level price and then seek to get customers to buy the higher specification model. A vehicle listed at £14,000 can easily increase to £25,000 for the top of the range.

4 The final way is simply to *charge more* for the same product; ie increase the price.

If you do not take the opportunity to maximize the sale at that point, the chances of that customer coming back to spend with you again are greatly reduced. If you are looking at option 1 above, there is a possibility that they may come back and buy the extra items when they need them, but there is always a risk that they may go somewhere else.

Consider a DIY person who wants to paint a room, and they are unsure of how much paint to buy. A website suggests it will be between 2 and 2.5 litres. A good paint sales assistant would offer, 'Buy the 2.5 litre tin, and an extra 0.5 litre tin just in case. If you don't open the second tin, bring it back for a full refund.' Many businesses offer this return policy knowing that statistically very few ever return things, even if they didn't actually use them. If they don't push at the initial sale, there are countless situations where a customer that didn't buy on the first visit, gets by and does not come back to buy on a second visit or for various reasons ends up buying from somewhere else.

In option 2, there remains some possibility that the customer will come back and buy these complementary items from you at some point, but there is a greater risk that they won't buy them at all or that they will shop somewhere else when they do decide they need them. If, for example, a salesperson fails to mention the extended warranty on the fridge we have just bought, the chances that we will actively seek out alternative cover from someone else, or even take up the offer from the insurance company's automated prompt letter that arrives a week later, is almost nil. For all sorts of products and services, if the opportunity to sell add-ons and extras is missed at the original point of sale, then it is lost forever.

Most importantly, if you are looking at option 3, a failure to up-sell to a higher-value option at the initial sale will lose the opportunity permanently. If the salesperson didn't persuade the customer to move from the entry-level car to a higher specification model, the odds on the customer coming back to upgrade are nil, because they will now already own the other model. With this kind of up-selling, you have one shot to get the value up.

What these examples demonstrate is the need to explore properly all of the up-selling and cross-selling options at the point of the initial sale. Some of these are clearly down to the skill of the salesperson to raise and explain the benefits of various options.

I have even heard salespeople start a pitch with the line, 'I guess you don't want the extended warranty option on this machine do you?'

Even if the customer might have taken up the warranty offer, it is highly unlikely that they would after that introduction!

Ouch!

However, getting customers to buy more of the same, complementary or higher-priced options is also driven by the prices of those options.

Using price to up-sell and cross-sell

If you can increase the overall value of the sale with extras or upgrades, you can afford to be flexible on price, since you will avoid the costs of trying to win a second sale, and the risk that you might permanently lose that opportunity.

So how do businesses do that?

There are a number of things that you could consider.

Let's look at a business selling, repairing and servicing garden equipment. This includes simple items such as hand pruners, spades, etc, and extends to lawnmowers, hedge trimmers, and to top-end items such as large ride-on mowers.

The customer wants a lawnmower but is undecided on the choice of machine. The salesperson should explore the key issues such as size of lawn area to be cut, whether it is level ground, has lots of shrubs, is close to an electricity supply, etc. Part of this is to establish the customer's needs, but it is also to get some indication of the customer's price threshold by showing top, middle and bottom options and gauging their reaction.

A good dialogue will narrow this down to just a few options for that customer to consider. Clearly the salesperson won't be able to sell higher volumes – the customer only needs one lawnmower – but selling extras or pushing for a higher quality and hence a higher-priced machine are still options.

This could boil down to offering a choice:

1 14" blade electric lawnmower, with two-year warranty and a 10 metre cable at £149.99;

2 16" push petrol mower with a two-year warranty for £299.99;

3 18" self-propelled cylinder petrol mower with two-year warranty for £759.99.

Assume that the business applies the same 40 per cent profit margin to all machines. This means that the profit from the one-off sale of these three options is around:

1 £60.

2 £120.

3 £304.

The business wants to sell the higher-value machine to generate a greater amount of profit. The salesperson will need to explain the features and benefits of each model, but can also consider a number of other issues. Let's also assume that all options would be OK for the customer and that it is therefore a genuine choice for them based on personal preferences, affordability and their assessment of value for money.

A petrol machine needs more looking after and the salesperson knows that few owners are diligent on maintenance and so there are often problems starting it the following year. Many therefore come back for a service. In short, the lifetime value of a customer will be much more with petrol machines than the cheaper electric one.

So how can he nudge the customer towards the higher-priced options?

What if the salesperson explained that every petrol mower came with a free *Petrol Mower Kit*, which includes:

- a litre of special mower engine oil (shelf price is £9.99);
- a free first-year service (normally £59.99);
- an under-mower cleaning kit (normally £12.99) (basically a stiff brush and metal scraper);
- a laminated A4 sheet with *How to maintain your petrol mower in peak condition* and *Safety tips for using a petrol mower* to stick on the inside of the shed (valued at £5.00).

As far as the customer knows, these items are valued at a total of almost £88. If you recall the Value Scales from last chapter, this free kit heaps a lot on the side of the customer's perception of value, and may well be enough to persuade the customer to choose either of the two petrol mowers rather than the electric one.

The salesperson could also suggest that if any customer buys a mower that costs more than £500, they will also get a free strimmer worth £100, which the salesperson knows only costs him £60 to buy.

Clearly, there are ways to build up packages that help to persuade each customer to spend a little more based on the increased value being provided with the higher-priced options.

Now look at this from the business's perspective.

If the business is prepared to offer a free £88 kit with any petrol mower, why don't they just reduce the price of the mower by this amount, and perhaps some customers will buy all those parts anyway? There are two issues. First, as explained above, many customers don't buy these extras at the point of sale, and won't come back later. Second, it doesn't cost the business £88 to deliver them.

Let's look at the value and cost of each component:

Item	Cost to deliver	Value to the customer
Oil	£5.00	£9.99
Free first service	£20.00	£59.99
Cleaning kit	£4.00	£12.99
Maintenance tips and safety sheet	£1.00	£5.00
Total	£30.00	£87.97

If the customer chooses the top machine, this generates a gross profit of £304, so that with the cost of the free kit (at £30), and with a free strimmer (at £60), there is still more profit in this choice than in any of the others.

> It is always better to make the Value Scales tip by adding more value, than by simply reducing the price.

A welding-supplies business developed a package with consumables and safety gear that came free (or at a special price) only when a customer bought the higher-value welder. The objective was to add high value to the customer's side of the Value Scales but at smaller cost, rather than just knocking the price down to make the sale.

In creating these bundles they identified a whole bunch of slow-moving stuff on the shelves, with some split packages or with cosmetic damage. After some deliberation, they created a *Surprise extras* box. This included £100 worth of welding-related items that would come free with the higher value machines. The small print confirmed that all the contents were able to be used for general welding or specifically for the machine being bought (ie it wasn't junk). However, it was a *surprise*, and the customer did not know what was included until after they had bought their machine.

What was the cost to the business?

The usual margin on consumables and safety equipment was 35 per cent, so the cost of these items was a maximum of £65, although the customer perceived them to be worth £100. However, it was better than that. Clearly the items they chose to put in the surprise box were the things that had been sat on the shelves for a long time, and which were in danger of becoming obsolete. It was quite possible that they would have a problem shifting them at all, and hence the real cost of giving them away was very little. They estimated that the real cost was no more than £25.

The result was a perception of the value of this bundle at £100, at a cost to the business of only £25.

Customers loved the idea. They all liked the surprise element, and the fact that it was £100 worth of goods for free, and it was therefore often enough to nudge them over the edge to buy the more expensive machine options without the need to discount the price of that machine.

Microsoft is another company with a number of bundled packages. The Office suite of products includes well-known components such as Word, Excel, PowerPoint and OneNote. Customers could opt to buy these as standalone versions of the software for £80 each, alternatively they could buy the whole suite of Office programs for just £100.

What every customer does is to add up the component prices and see that the whole suite would cost almost £290, compared to the bundle for just £100.

Even more interesting is that Microsoft offers a bundle that includes three copies of the whole suite of programmes for just

£90; ie it is £10 *cheaper* to buy three copies than it is to buy just the one.

So why would Microsoft do this? Clearly Microsoft invests huge amounts in developing their software, but once they have this, the actual cost of delivery is negligible. In fact all the programs can be downloaded rather than shipped on disc, so delivery cost of one or a dozen items is essentially nil. They know that many families own a number of PCs and laptops and that if the software was expensive, they might only have the Office suite on one machine for work or homework, using the others just for browsing the internet, social media or gaming. Therefore offering a bundle of three copies is attractive to many customers.

In fact, a review of the Microsoft website shows a huge number of bundles that customers can opt for, with every option showing a bundle with that item matched with something else.

The whole point of bundling is to maximize the value of the sale to the customer at the point of the initial sale, so that opportunity for extras does not walk out of the door when the customer does. The key is that businesses are prepared to be more flexible on price when customers buy higher volumes, additional items or higher specification items because there is more profit to be made out of the overall sale. If they can actually hold their prices and add value through adding-in low cost but high value extras to the sale, even better.

What Microsoft have done is to set their prices for the bundles they want to sell at a price that they know will make them a good profit and be good value for money to the customer, and then uplifted substantially the cost of each component of the bundle to make the bundle look exceptional value for money. Do they ever sell a standalone version of Word? Probably not.

There is another aspect to the issue of bundling.

Offering choices increases the value of the sale

When you look at all sorts of businesses you will see that they often bundle things into three simple options for customers to choose.

These may be differentiated by higher-value components, in which case the language can be:

- Gold;
- Silver;
- Bronze.

Or they differentiate based on the quantity of the item:

- Small;
- Medium;
- Large.

Although even this has evolved into:

- Standard;
- Large;
- Supersized.

There are even some businesses that offer bundles that are not based on quality or scale, but just on a different range of choices, such as the Sky deals where a basic entertainment pack can be upgraded with:

- Sky Movies;
- Sky Sports;
- Sky Entertainment Extra.

Or Orange Mobile offering bundles called Dolphin, Canary, Panther, Racoon and Camel!

What all of these bundling options are seeking to do is to nudge the customer into spending a little bit more each time, as each upgrade option seems like better value for money; ie the more you spend the more you save.

There has been a lot of research into how offering choice affects customers' spending habits, so let's start with a simple choice of Gold, Silver or Bronze. The idea is that it will be obvious to each potential customer that as you move up from Bronze to Silver and then Gold, the service levels, quality or range of elements in each option will increase, but so too will the price.

Of course there should be a price differential, as Silver and Gold options will cost more to deliver and are of greater value to the customer, but there is also an underlying psychology as to why people will choose each level.

You probably know of someone who when given choices of Gold, Silver or Bronze, would choose Gold by virtue of the fact that it is the most expensive and therefore assumed to be the best option available, irrespective of the apparent value for money of that choice. Buying the top option is a statement about them. There are some customers where the cost simply doesn't matter as they have enough money so that this individual spending decision has no impact on them, so that they buy Gold just because they can't be bothered to think about the price/value issues for a comparatively small spend for them; ie like asking a millionaire to choose Gold, Silver or Bronze car-cleaning products that are priced from £20 to £40.

You may also know a good number of people who would always choose Bronze for the same, but opposite, reason; ie they are inherently price-sensitive *cheap* customers that adopt a *make-do* approach to all their spending decisions; or there are those that can only afford the entry-level option irrespective of the value for money that Silver or Gold may offer.

If you do nothing else than to offer several choices where the increase in the cost of delivering the product or service is matched exactly with an increase in the price charged, you will find a proportion of your customers buy Gold, some Silver and the rest buy Bronze.

Offer only one price level based on one simple product or service offering, and you may well miss out on customers at either end of the spectrum. Like a one-size-fits-all clothing policy where you are forced to buy the largest size so that people can at least wear the clothes, offer *standard* price only, and you are usually forced down to the lowest price that is acceptable to all or most of the customers you deal with. When this happens and you allow yourself to set your prices low, you make less profit from the Silver- or Gold-style customers you almost certainly have somewhere in your customer list. Alternatively, if you stick with one standard price and set it too high, you may lose some of your Bronze ones altogether. By offering multiple levels you have a chance to hit the spot and maximize profit from a wider cross-section of your customer base.

If you do offer multiple price levels, this will involve each higher level having extra value elements at an extra cost. Let's just ignore the actual costs differential of the options and consider where you should set the price points for Silver and Gold to differentiate them from Bronze? Lots of research into this area has concluded a number of interesting points.

Alternative price options affect the perception of value of all options

If any option is priced highly, the perception of the value for money of the lower-priced options increases. Let's say that your one-size-fits-all *standard* price would have been £100, and you surveyed 1,000 customers on whether they thought £100 represented good value for money, you might get 500 to agree that it was. If you now offer an option of a Gold price at £300, Silver at £200, and Bronze at £100, and you then asked another 1,000 customers the same question of whether Bronze represented good value for money, you might now get 750 say that it was.

The only difference is that the customer is no longer making an assessment of value from a single price option, but seeing £100 in context with two much higher alternative prices. It simply appears to be better value than the other options.

But if the Gold and Silver options were set at £120 and £110, then Bronze would seem poorer value by comparison, and many would consider upgrading. So perhaps only 250 of our 1,000 surveyed customers would see Bronze as value for money.

Our customers' perception of value, and hence their willingness to buy, is directly affected by any comparison to alternative options we offer them.

JN Boat Supplies Limited

Setting price differentials properly

So how do you set the prices of each option?

Let's start with a situation where each level matches an increase in value with the increase in price. Bronze is £100. Silver is twice the price of Bronze at £200, and is twice as valuable (by most customers' assessment). Gold is three times the price of Bronze at £300 and three times as good. That is, Silver and Gold are not *better* deals, just inclusive of more elements at fairly increased prices.

The decision for each customer is therefore predominantly affected by their natural bias towards the Gold, Silver or Bronze options that they would normally default to, based on affordability, the significance of the spend to them or their natural bias as *high spenders* or *cheap* customers.

There are several things they could try:

- Increase the price of the entry-level choice; ie increase the price of Bronze to say £150. This would have the impact of making Silver and Gold options seem much better value for money, and perhaps nudge a few Bronze customers to upgrade, or it would simply generate more profit on those customers. It could, however, price a few customers out altogether. The Microsoft Office suite example above is exactly this. In reality they may have been prepared to sell the Word program on its own for £20, but by pushing this to £80 (and similar prices for all the other standalone programs) they make their bundled prices seem exceptional value. There are, of course, few alternatives to the Microsoft products so they have a bit more confidence that customers will upgrade rather than leave.

- They could reduce the price of Gold and Silver to be nearer to Bronze; say £275 and £175 respectively. This would have the same impact of making both options appear to be much better value for money, as they probably actually are. The decision for the seller is whether making a smaller profit margin is acceptable as it is still actually a bigger amount than they make on Bronze; ie where they used to make £50, £100 and £150 profit on Bronze, Silver and Gold, they now only make £50,

£75 and £125, respectively. If they saw a good number of customers move up the levels, they may well be prepared to accept this lower percentage but higher amount.

- They could move the Silver price slightly up or down. If they nudge up the price of Silver they may make a little more profit from those that didn't want Bronze but wouldn't pay Gold price; or they could drop it slightly to nudge a few Bronze customers to upgrade because the perceived value for money is greater.

So which is the right answer?

Every business will be unique, and the value elements it can offer to create multiple options will vary enormously. When you try to develop multiple options, you will be amazed at which customers will upgrade and which ones don't, and at how much various customers will or won't pay to move. This goes back to the point made in some of the earlier chapters, which is the need to do some research into what your customers want, and what your competitors are offering.

It does involve some trial and error to establish what the perfect position for you is as the business owner or CEO/director. Only by testing can you find the place where you capture maximum value from your naturally Gold customers, but still keep the Silver and Bronze ones at prices that work for you and for them.

However, here are the critical issues:

- There must be some visible differentiation of the product and service that reflects broadly the price differentials you set; ie you cannot set Gold price at £100 more than Silver if the only obvious difference is a free pen that costs £5. However, as covered later, it is more often *you* that sets the expectation of value, for example by saying *the price includes installation, which is normally charged at £75.*

  When you look at how you bundle up your products and services into multiple levels, make sure that the differences are explained well and that the *value* offered broadly reflects the extra price.

- Ideally, the gap between the top two options should be smaller than that between the bottom two. Again, each business will be unique and each bundle include different things, but if you can offer a range and flex prices as you wish, then you really want the decision to upgrade from Silver to Gold to be easier than the decision to upgrade from Bronze to Silver.

- When people assess value for money of a product or service, they often need some sort of benchmark against which to judge. If you offer only one option, then on many occasions that benchmark will be a comparison with another business, and hence increase your risk of an unfavourable comparison. If you offer your customers three choices, they are subconsciously lulled into making their assessment of value based on a comparison of your offers alone. Which one they choose is less important to you than the fact that they are at least choosing one of yours. Many businesses develop packages to include the obvious extras that the customer will need anyway such as consumables, or an annual service, and which customers simply don't consider at the point of the initial purchase. When these issues are explained during the selling process, the customer is left with a feeling that perhaps the alternative supplier is either hiding something, hasn't explained the sale very well, or may just assume that all of that alternative supplier's extras are likely to be expensive. Offering three choices rather than one will increase your chances of any sale, and quite probably of a larger or more profitable one for you.

- Having an expensive option makes the other options seem much better value for money. A restaurant had a range of choices for main courses between £15 and £25. As you would expect, they sold fewer of the £25 meals than they did of the cheaper options. They then added a £35 menu item and monitored sales over the following six months. They sold very few of the now most expensive meals at £35, but they did sell many more of the £25 option. All that had changed was that the £25 option became seemingly better value when compared to the new £35 top choice.

> MSL computers limited has developed a *Platinum* service level that they
> never expect to sell, but whose only purpose is to make the previously
> top-priced option of Gold, seem better value by comparison.

Although there may be merit in having four, five, six or even more
options on the basis that the more offers you have the greater the
chance that one will hit the spot perfectly with each customer,
research has suggested that even just four choices can be enough to
confuse customers into not making any choice at all. Most people are
able to understand very quickly the idea of *Gold*, *Silver* and *Bronze*
or, *Supersize*, *Large* and *Standard*, and find it easy to place themselves
quickly into the category they naturally fit whether Top, Middle
or Bottom. So if you are starting to consider how you can package
what you do into bundles, stick with just three to start with.

The price of pain

Part of the purpose of bundling is to try and find a better way of
making the Value Scales balance than taking the easy option of
simply discounting the price. As a supplier you will usually be
prepared to be more flexible on the deal if the customer is spending
more, so if you can add bigger bundles on the customer's side of
the scales you can afford to adjust your prices to make the scales tip
or to add value greater than the cost of supply.

But it is a little more complicated than that as each option to add
extra value into these bundles rarely has the same costs to supply.
What businesses need to consider is the impact on them of each
option they can use to make the scales tip, the more expensive the
option is to deliver, the greater the pain for them as the supplier.

This issue is known as the *Price of Pain*.

You will recall that in Chapter 2 we talked about the Pleasure and
Pain Principle; ie that buying decisions are made based on achieving
pleasure or avoiding pain. What a supplier should be aiming to do is

to add maximum pleasure to the customer's side of the Value Scales for the lowest pain on their own side.

Return to the example of the welding supplies company. A customer wants to buy a new machine with a list price of £1,000, but knows that there is a deal to be had. The various possible outcomes and the level of pain associated with each are listed below, in the order of the most to the least painful.

TABLE 6.1

The deal	Customer pleasure	Supplier pain
Sale at £1,000 price with a 'standard' trade discount of 20%	**£200** less to pay	**£200** less income
Sale at £1,000 price but bundled with a basket of 'FREE' extra goods with a list price of £200	Bonus **£200** worth of extra goods	Cost of extra goods at say **£150**
Sale at £1,000 price with a 'FREE' year's service agreement normally charged at £200	Bonus of **£200** of added value	Real cost of service at say **£100** of labour
Sale at £1,000 price with free on-site training and annual telephone support	Bonus of **£200** of added value	Real cost of service at say **£50** of labour
Sale at £1,000 price but with clearer explanation of the value of the product and benefits of dealing with the company	Greater confidence in the fairness of the the deal	Extra time to achieve the sale at say **£25**

As you can see from the options above, indiscriminate giving of discounts is by far the most painful option, and this is explained in great depth in Chapter 10. A discount of £200 is £200 less sales income, £200 less profit, £200 less cash to be collected, and ultimately £200 less money in the bank.

The price of discounts is pound for pound pain for the supplier.

Ouch!

Simply taking the time to sell properly, explaining the features and benefits, and handling objections, payment terms, delivery schedules, etc is by far the cheapest option of them all. However, most businesses start at the most expensive option of discounting, not the cheapest of selling better. If they started at selling better, and worked through the other options of free training, free servicing, free extra goods or whatever are the additional offers they could bundle into the deal, only giving real discounts off the price as a last resort, the average costs of making the deal happen would reduce substantially.

The key is that bundling your products and services into compelling offers that encourage the customer to spend more, appreciate the value of the features and benefits that you offer, and that allow you to add the items that have high value to the customer at lower cost to you, will make your overall profit will increase considerably.

Summary

Offering your customers choice will improve your chances of making a sale, although this does require some selling skill to explain and persuade customers to upgrade. If all you do is ensure that your salespeople explain the features and benefits of what you do, better than they do at the moment, sales will increase.

If that choice can be clearly identified as bundles that offer entry-level, mid-level and top-level options, then many customers will naturally gravitate to their preferred option, and some of these will be Silver- or Gold-level customers.

This will enable you to sell extras and add-ons that would in all probability be lost sales if they are simply other products or services that the customer must seek out, or even if they are extras that you point out to them as separately priced options at the initial point of sale.

You need to quantify the pain threshold for you of giving discounts versus the alternatives of bundling extras into competitively priced deals where you add high value but where the cost of delivery for you is less.

Action points

1 Do research into how other businesses use bundles to sell their products and services. This should include:

   - Speak to some managers in other businesses you know (not your competitors) and ask them what bundles they have. Identify their Gold, Silver and Bronze levels, and look for any Platinums.

   - Investigate your competitors' websites and see what bundles they have that could apply to your products and services.

   - Take a walk around your local retail businesses (DIY stores, computer retailers, etc) and note down all of the bundles they use, how these are expressed and priced.

2 Now, get your pricing team of sales, production and finance people to design various bundles that you could offer reflecting increasing levels of value. Set price points for each bundle.

3 Have your salespeople test these options on a few trusted customers, refining the offering as appropriate.

4 Have the team develop training materials to explain the new bundles and present them properly to a wider range of new and existing customers. Organize training for all salespeople to present the new approach. This must include specific training in how to lead the customer into an upgrade, not just to explain the bundles available.

5 Finally, have the finance people monitor the results from these various new offers so that you can reassess the price points and monitor the additional profits flowing from the rollout of the bundles.

Customers don't always want the cheapest

Many business owners and managers feel that they are under constant pressure from customers to reduce their prices. Sometimes this is nothing more than a subconscious and unfounded fear of negative customer reactions, which we have considered in previous chapters. Sometimes it is explicit pressure from customers actually asking for lower prices, or threatening to leave, although this is usually only a small segment of customers rather than being representative of the whole lot. Most times it is just the normal request for a better deal as customers test the boundaries and seek to check that they are getting a fair deal.

This means that the last thing on many business owners' minds is to actually increase their prices as there is a very real fear that the result will be lost customers. The challenge for all is to know when these fears are real and when they are not.

This chapter covers the myth that increasing prices *automatically* means losing customers, by addressing these key concerns.

This chapter includes just one key learning point:

- Increasing prices doesn't automatically mean losing customers.

Increasing prices doesn't automatically mean losing customers

If a business is serious about profit improvement, it will invariably at some point involve consideration of a price increase. However, as

explained above, business owners and managers are invariably resist-
ant to this, and impetus to change must often come from an outsider
– a trusted friend in another business or a consultant.

Whoever is advising the business, their detached assessment of the
merits of a price increase will most often be met with the response:

> No, I *can't* put the price up, it is the *only* thing customers care about
> and I will lose them if I do.'

Are their customers really that price sensitive, or is it simply that
these owners and managers are untrained in pricing issues? The
reality is that most customers are nowhere near as price sensitive as
we believe they are. A few examples will illustrate this.

> Business owners and managers are too close to their own businesses to
> be sufficiently detached from the price issue. They need to explore their
> buying habits in other areas of their lives and then put themselves in the
> shoes of the majority of their customers. Otherwise their judgements are
> too tainted by just a small number of painful experiences with their own
> customers.
>
> Ouch!

Q1 How did you decide on the last car you bought?

When anyone considers why they chose the make and model of car
they drive they will produce a number of quite valid reasons:

- I have always owned Fords.
- I needed one with a bit of space as I have four kids and a dog.
- I do around 70,000 kilometres per year so need one that is
  really comfortable.
- The garage was just around the corner so it's convenient.
- My brother works at the dealership.
- It has all the gadgets I wanted or ones unique to that model.
- My family likes the colour.

- It's for business and needs to show a certain image to customers.

In fact, whether consciously or subconsciously, there are dozens of individual elements to our decision to buy any particular make and model of car. It is a combination of some practical elements and some purely emotional ones. The key point is that when we have gone out to buy what is for most people the second biggest item of expenditure they ever buy, very few buyers make an exclusively price-driven decision and buy the cheapest option available. Whether you spend £50,000 or just £500 on your car, you can be certain that there were cheaper options out there. Price is of course part of the equation, and certainly we cannot spend more than we can afford, but that is simply one of a very long list of factors all put into the melting pot to form a decision. Some customers may be shopping in the used car lot with sticker prices of £999 to £3,999, and some may be in the luxury car showroom with sticker prices of £25,999 to £75,999, but within these affordability bands they still have the choice to spend more or less as they decide. When they have narrowed the choice down to a particular make, model, specification and colour of car, they may then look hard to ensure there are not identical options out there at a lower price. However, it is not a price-driven decision for most buyers.

Ask the average car salesperson, 'How many people walk out of the showroom spending their original budget or less?' They will tell you that it is a fraction of the numbers of people who completely blew the budget when faced with the highly polished car of their dreams screaming *buy me!* as they walked in.

A key element of the buying decision for cars is the emotional, or perhaps better named aspirational purchase. We buy it for what we believe it may help us become: how we look compared to our neighbours, or our subconscious aspiration to be the funky young couple in the TV ad.

So how do car manufacturers set their prices? Well they do a lot of upfront research and market testing. They use comparisons with other cars in their fleet to see where the new model sits, and with other brands to see who they would be competing against. And they absolutely know to the penny what it costs to make. But when push comes to shove, they just use their judgement as to what they may be able to get away with.

As previously covered, there is a danger with just *guessing* a number as you may set it too low and have excess demand and lower profits, or you may go too high and not sell enough.

One of the *tricks of the trade* on pricing that car dealers selling new cars excel at is the 'Base Price Plus' approach. What they do is advertise and promote an entry-level price for say a Ford Focus at £14,000. This compares favourably with similar-sized cars from other manufacturers. The problem for the dealer is that they make very little profit on this sale, in fact it may often only be a few hundred pounds. However, when the customer looks at the specification of the basic car they often opt to buy a higher specification model, or find a good number of extras that they would like on their car.

The advantage for the dealer is that many of these optional extras attract a significantly higher profit margin than the purchase of the car itself. How many customers do you think buy the base-level car at the advertised low price and add no extras? My guess is none. What this all tells us in answer to the question of *everyone wants the lowest price, don't they?* is that when it comes to cars the answer is an emphatic *No!*

There are many elements to the buying decision, of which price is clearly one, although this may be better phrased as *affordability* rather than purely a price issue. What it also shows is another very critical point in pricing. Not all customers are the same!

The reason that there are so many variants is that each customer will have some factors that are more important to them than other factors. A young man buying his first new car may well have a lower budget for the core price of the car, and hence buy the basic model, but he may then place a far higher value on the benefits of the Bose sound system than he might on having a towbar as an optional extra. The couple with young children may have the budget for a higher basic specification model, and may then place higher value on rear seat DVD players or the easy-to-wipe-down leather seat upgrade.

By offering so many variants and then a host of optional extras, the car dealers are able to offer almost individual pricing to each customer, delivering a uniquely tailored product to maximize this price.

Now, the uniqueness of customers does not just occur when they are buying cars. Every customer you have is unique, and will place different emphasis on different elements of the product or services you sell.

We will return to cars later because they provide many other good examples of pricing strategies, as they are very expensive items and in industries where manufacturers have spent millions researching the buying habits and decision-making processes to work out how to squeeze as much money out of us as they can.

It is fair to conclude that when we look at cars from the perspective of the customer, we do not simply look for the cheapest option.

Q2 Why do you choose the supermarket that you shop at?

Once again the same question will elicit a whole range of answers and reasons. There are bound to be some readers who are up-market Waitrose customers, some will be middle market Tesco or Sainsbury's customers, and some might shop at low-cost brands such as Aldi or Lidl. Thus for very similar items of groceries, shoppers are choosing upmarket, mid-range or low-cost stores with prices that reflect this choice.

A typical basket of shopping will cost more at some stores than it does at others. The television is swamped with advertising campaigns from most major supermarkets where they promise to be the cheapest or give money back plus 10 per cent or using other similarly brave price-match deals. So it would appear that the supermarkets believe it is all about price. In actual fact what they are trying to do is to get the customer in the front door with price promotions on what are only a relatively small number of common products customers buy. Once they have you in store, there are a million other items they want to persuade you to buy.

Let's just look at a few of their techniques:

- Have you been to a store with an in-house bakery? These activities make very little profit compared to the value of the space they take up in retail sales terms. So why have them? Because when we are stimulated to feel hungry we spend more money. These stores deliberately feed the smells of the bakery back into the stores when they could just as easily extract them to remove the smells and save energy. We buy to satisfy a basic need for food, and the store works very hard to stimulate that urge to its advantage.

- When you check out you will almost always have to wait a few minutes in the queue at the till. What is right there in front of you? Impulse buys. Magazines, sweets, bottles of wine. Low-value items that many customers just drop into the basket at the last minute. Couldn't the store have *slicker checkouts* with more people and more space to put trolleys? Well they could, but they don't want to. Typical customers can add £s to the shopping bill between finishing the shop and actually getting to the cashier at the till to pay, just stood waiting in line.

- Asda pioneered the use of *greeters*. These were smiley people who stood at the door and said *hello* or *good morning* as people walked in. This was part of the policy of great customer service, and included an aspect of spotting for shoplifters. But what they proved was that customers who received a great welcome spent more money. They measured average spend per customer when the greeters were on duty and it was always higher than when they were not. If the customer is happy, they will probably spend more, and be less sensitive about the price. Unhappy customers are less likely to buy, and certainly more likely to challenge on the price.

What these examples demonstrate is that our buying decisions are not just price led. The chemical reactions to smells and taste can stimulate more sales. The engineering of places to encourage impulse buys, and simply getting customers into the right frame of mind to spend money can all increase the average spend.

It is important to note, however, that supermarkets do all have a distinct advantage. The majority buy in such huge volumes, and at such competitive prices, that they are able to sell at very low margins. Later chapters will explode some of the myths we have all come to believe on supermarket pricing.

However, just stand back from the detail of individual stores or TV price promotions, and you can see that across this market, some customers buy in bargain discount stores whether through financial need or their own personal judgement of value for money, while many others shop in increasingly expensive stores based on factors that are more important to them.

These factors will include:

- convenience – a store closer to their home or work place;
- product range – using a larger store that may have everything you need;
- opening hours – using the 24-hour stores because you work nights;
- brand loyalty – Tesco Clubcard members who accumulate points.

One more issue on price as the decision-maker in supermarkets:

Tesco advertise a *tin of beans for only £0.26p*. If you do decide to shop at Tesco, and you are looking to buy a simple tin of baked beans, there are actually 46 different options that you could choose. These include four-packs, fridge packs, and single-person tins, one of which is indeed only £0.26p.

To ensure we make a clear comparison, let's just look at a single tin of beans of around 400 grams in weight. Some brands are 415 grams and some are 420 grams, so we will just look at these tins using the pence per kilogram figure to get a real price comparison.

The cheapest option is the 'Tesco Everyday Value Baked Beans in Tomato Sauce 420 g' at a cost of £0.26 or £0.62 per kilogram. The most expensive is 'Heinz Baked Beans 415 g' at a cost of £0.70 or £1.69 per kilogram. Now you may simply believe that the Heinz product is better quality and hence worth three times the price, and you may see that with every one of the 46 options that customers can choose, whether including sausages, using organically grown beans, or because the brand suggests better-quality ingredients.

The point is simple. Some customers will spend more money on a variation of the same product for whatever reason motivates them to do so. Although Tesco may promote the fact that their beans are only £0.26 a tin, very few of the customers will actually buy this option just because it is the cheapest.

This principle applies to many businesses in many sectors. They promote the very low-priced entry level or basic product, but in reality very few customers actually buy this bottom end option. So while the perception of low price may well entice some customers to come in in the first place, it is rarely the sole element of the buying decision.

Q3 Which plumber would you choose?

Your washing machine has gone wrong and your laundry room is flooded. You know from experience or recommendation that there are four possible options for a plumber you could call. These are:

FIGURE 7.1

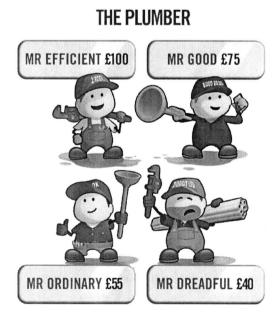

Mr Efficient is an excellent plumber. He answers calls immediately, is there in an hour, and has any parts he might need in his van. He discusses whether to repair or replace the machine. The repair is done quickly, he tests the machine to ensure the problem is solved and cleans up the mess. He invoices on the spot and confirms his work is 100 per cent guaranteed.

Mr Efficient charges £100 for the work.

Mr Dreadful didn't answer until a second call. He promised to come that morning but arrived the following day, only after another call. He suggested it was probably the motor, and disappeared for an hour to get one. He replaced the motor, left the old one, lots of mess and said he only took cash.

Mr Dreadful's bill was only £40.

The other two options were variations of these, with Mr Ordinary being slightly better than Mr Dreadful but costing a little more at £55, and Mr Good being better again but costing £75.

How would you choose a plumber in this situation? What impact would each of the following elements have on your decision?

- speed of response;
- turning up when they say they will;
- holding spares on the van to avoid leaving to get them;
- consultation regarding the repairs vs replacement decision;
- speed of work done;
- testing the machine on completion;
- cleaning up afterwards;
- doing the paperwork and invoicing properly;
- the guarantee over the work done.

Obviously Mr Efficient does all the right things and Mr Dreadful does the absolute minimum.

Which one would you select?

In most situations of this type you will see around 20 per cent opting for the top price offer, 35 per cent for the next level, 25 per cent for the third level, and the balance of around 20 per cent choosing the cheapest option. The reality is that most of us are more concerned about the plumber actually turning up on time and doing a reliable job than we are about saving a few pounds.

The balance of these options depends on factors that are unique to each customer, such as whether they need to take time off work, or have a whole football team's kit to wash for the following day. But in most cases the only customers that choose the cheapest option are those that are constrained by their budget. It is not therefore a value-for-money decision, just the fact that they don't have the money to choose the more expensive options.

In this example there is only a small percentage of customers for whom it is truly an issue of being the lowest price. The vast majority of customers will pay more for a service that fits their personal issues of speed, reliability, etc. That principle is true of any marketplace.

> Don't allow your prices to be set based on the bottom, price-sensitive section of your customer base.

A major player in the electrical wholesale industry did a Europe-wide survey of their customers to find out the factors most important to them in the buying decision. This was the largest survey in that industry – ever.

They got a great deal of information, and boiled it down to the conclusion that their customers wanted three things (in this order):

1 on-time delivery (it must be delivered when it was promised);

2 availability of stock (a wide range and available on demand, so that they can get hold of core products instantly);

3 value for money (not price).

Note that price was the third thing on the list not the first, and that it was not simply the price itself but what the customer perceived to be the value for money, that was their concern.

What do these examples prove?

There are many factors, both consciously and subconsciously considered, in people's buying decisions. Very rarely do we as customers go for the cheapest option simply because it is the cheapest. Why is it then that when we are setting our own prices, we completely ignore this and assume that our own customers are solely price led? It simply isn't true.

> The problem is that unless we make it clear to our customers what all the other factors that they could and should be considering are, then price is the only information they have with which to make their decision.
>
> TR – Micro Software Limited

If price is the only data that customers have then that is what they will base their decision on. In fact, if a customer looks at your products or services against those of your competitors, and there is no other information on which they can base their decision but price, they would be mad to buy what they believe to be an identical item for more money. If you want customers to pay a little more, you need to help them see the difference between your options and those of any alternative suppliers.

Businesses that are large enough to have many teams of salespeople out looking for new business or managing customer relationships can do an exercise to list all of the great things they can say about their own company, to tease out reasons why customers should buy from them. Typically this uncovers things such as:

- reliability of products;
- friendly service;
- established reputation;
- a 'We care' attitude.

There can be dozens of these *fluffy* expressions which suggest that the business is simply a *nice* place to work and to do business with.

Digging deeper reveals more specific details:

- money-back guarantees;
- extended credit facilities;
- free delivery;
- 24-hour emergency call out;
- access to technical expertise;
- online account management;
- same-day delivery within 120 kilometres;
- direct-dial access to own account manager;
- free loan machine until we can source a replacement.

This list often includes some really valuable elements to the service that the business provides to its customers. What is most illuminating is that none of these things are recorded in the company's sales literature, often not shown on the website, and almost never discussed by the salesperson with the customer.

Now if we go back to the chapter covering the Value Scales you will remember that in the absence of these value-added elements, our only negotiating tool becomes lowering the price.

It's quite simple really.

> If *you* make price the big issue, then it will be the big issue.

You need to help your customers to make a judgement about the value to them of the various features and benefits of the product or service you are offering, and explain all the other great reasons they should do business with you. If you fail to do this then the only data left on which they can base their decision is the price.

What we all know as customers is that we are prepared to spend more on better quality or on better service where we:

- understand what the features and benefits are;

- are able to place our own values on those elements that are important to us; and

- have choice to add in or take out elements as we wish.

It is clearly critical to ensure that customers understand all the positive reasons to do business with you in order to help you defend the prices you charge (or may want to in future). However, there is a minor issue of the chicken or egg variety to consider.

Should you get price on the table straight away and then run through all of the features, benefits and reasons to buy, or should you cover all these points and only cover price right at the end?

The most important point is that you do it at all. There are thousands of businesses that offer exceptional service and products of the highest quality that compete solely on price with competitors who are nowhere near their standards.

We found that the best option is to have four to six key points to explain to the customer *before* price is even mentioned, and only then to put a number on the table. Before the customer responds you should then have one extra thing to add that seems to be a special offer to them.

CP – Active Games Limited

This may go something like:

Before I tell you the price of that lawnmower, can I just let you know a couple of important points? We are the largest independent retailer of lawnmowers in the area, and we have grown almost exclusively from reputation and repeat customers, by making sure we give our customers exactly what they need. We only buy our products from carefully selected manufacturers where we are completely satisfied on the reliability and durability of the machines they offer. Every machine is checked before we ship it to the customer to make sure all the parts are included, so that there are no annoying problems when a nut or cable is missing as you sometimes get with the online discount stores. We offer an extended two-year guarantee as we are really confident about the quality of all the machines we sell.

The price of the mower you want is £795 including VAT.

But I tell you what, if you take the mower today, I will also deliver the machine to you already assembled, fuelled and tested to ensure that it starts first time.

Whether plumbing, lawnmowers, or any other product or service, each business needs to work out what their key points are and develop the right approach to get them across. If you do this well, then I have no doubt that you will quickly discover that price is only part of the decision-making process, not the only element.

Summary

In the majority of cases it simply isn't true that people buy the cheapest option. They either consciously or unconsciously consider many other factors to weigh up the overall decision to buy or not buy something.

You need to establish what those factors are for your products or services and then explain them better, build them into your selling and marketing processes, and work on improving them so that they are better than your competitors.

Those businesses that have developed a clear selling message that includes elements such as availability, reliability, customer service, speed of delivery, etc, have made price a less important issue.

Price really isn't the big issue:

We *pretend* it is.

Action points

1 Look at all the things you bought in the recent past and ask yourself the question:

> Was that the cheapest option available, or did I consider (consciously or subconsciously) other factors such as convenience, quality, availability, branding, etc?

Consider items such as:

- petrol (convenience rather than price);
- cola (brand loyalty or subconscious response to the marketing);
- trades services such as plumber or electrician (speed of response or reliability);
- restaurant (reputation, atmosphere, location);
- electrical appliance (safety/reliability or response to marketing);
- professional advice, eg accountant or lawyer (established expertise or reputation);
- medical services, eg dentist or physiotherapist (clean hygienic environment or caring personal service).

Look through your cheque stubs or credit card receipts and look at the value of any items where you believe price was the deciding factor, and the value of all other payments where there may have been a number of other factors in the decision.

Quantify the value of your spending that is truly price led and compare this with your spending where price was just part of the equation.

2 Once you have considered what matters to you as a customer on these various spending situations, get the pricing team assembled in earlier chapters to do the same exercise on their own spending habits, and then to look at your business and brainstorm all the other positive reasons that customers might do business with you.

3 Get that list marshalled into order of importance and consider how they apply to each of your top 20 products. Make sure they are well promoted in your sales material and covered in the sales conversations with every customer.

4 Get your frontline salespeople to discuss the following key issues and agree a clear plan of how they are incorporated into your selling processes:

– How do you maximize value from each possible sale? That is, what questions are asked to up-sell or cross-sell other products or services?

– What impulse buys can you prompt your customers to make? How are these promoted at the point of sale; whether at the till, sales counter or in the sales meeting?

– What steps do you take to ensure that your customers are in the best frame of mind to spend money with you? Consider how they are greeted into your business, how they are looked after if they are waiting, and the standards of customer service they will experience.

Exploding all of the myths about pricing

The views of business owners, CEOs, directors and managers of pricing techniques have been formed by what they see being done elsewhere or in many cases based on a form of urban myth. They often haven't undertaken any research on the subject, read any books or engaged any experts to assist them in understanding this critical subject, in the way that they may well have done to get a grip on other business areas, such as employment law for example.

This chapter looks specifically at some of the myths that surround the way businesses set prices, and it will change your attitude completely.

This chapter includes:

- Myth: Customers only want the cheapest.
- Myth: Loss leaders work.
- Myth: A 50 per cent off sale is a 50 per cent off sale.
- Myth: Presentation of the price doesn't matter.
- Myth: All prices should end in a '9'.
- Myth: The best person to set the price is the salesperson.
- Myth: Setting prices is a once a year decision.
- Myth: Every customer is worth having and every sale matters.
- Myth: Raising prices loses customers.

Myth: Customers only want the cheapest

This is the biggest myth of them all, and the whole of the previous chapter covered it in detail. (If you jumped Chapter 7, go back and read it now.)

There are further myths to consider. Key decision-makers often use terms such as *loss leaders* or *discount sales* without really understanding the financial implications of the strategies they design. Or they may have set prices based on their view of some psychological significance of numbers.

Myth: Loss leaders work

A wholesale business based in Bristol has a number of branches throughout the UK. Multi-branched businesses are great because it is possible to test the impact of a whole host of issues by comparing the outcomes at various branches doing different things. In single-location businesses it is just harder to compare two different strategies and measure the results.

The Bristol-based company had one particular branch that was notorious for selling certain core products at ridiculously low prices when others in the group were charging much more for the same products.

The argument put forward by the branch manager was that these were *loss leaders*. He believed that by selling these core products at very low prices, it encouraged customers to come in and buy them, and that they then went on to purchase other products. He figured that if his branch charged the same prices as the other branches in the group then his customers would vote with their feet and shop at competitors for *all* of their stuff.

The basic logic of this is sound. If by selling product A at very low prices we are able to create a volume of customers who then buy products B, C, D and so on, then it may well be worthwhile doing this. The key question of course is whether the profit created by selling these additional products was more or less than the profit given away on the so-called loss leaders.

Because they had the advantage of a large branch network, they were able to compare the volume of the *loss leader* items sold from branch to branch, and then to see whether the volumes of other products were higher in the branch using the *loss leader* approach or not.

They compared two similar-sized branches in Cardiff and Birmingham. Cardiff was charging £30 for a 50 metre box of electric cable, a standard fast-moving everyday product. Birmingham sold this same product for £20.

TABLE 8.1

	Cardiff branch	Birmingham branch
Selling price	£30	£20
Cost	£18	£18
Volume sold per month	100 boxes	200 boxes
Profit per month	£1,200	£400

The results showed that Birmingham generated only £400 – one third of the profit of Cardiff from twice the volume.

The question therefore is whether Birmingham was selling lots more of their other items on which it was generating additional profits and whether the extra profit from these items was more or less than the £800 it had given away by under-selling the cable.

They looked at the volume of cable sold by each of the various branches and compared this with the volume of a range of other products that the branch manager was convinced were selling better as a result of these special deals on cable. For simplicity, we compared the average results from all other branches to the results for Birmingham.

TABLE 8.2

Volume of items sold each month Product	Average of all other branches	Birmingham
Electric cable	110 boxes	200 boxes
Consumer units	54	48
Switch plates	423	442
Appliances	34	38
Alarm systems	15	12

The consistent result was that volumes of products sold by Birmingham were either barely above, or in some cases actually below, the average volumes achieved by the other branches selling cable at the normal higher price. It simply wasn't true that the customers attracted in by the extremely low price of the cable were then spending money on other things while they were there. The conclusion, which was tested in a number of other ways, was that the customers were indeed attracted to the low price of the cable, but that this was having little or no impact on the volume of other products sold. They even found some customers who, when asked, confirmed that they often came in just to buy the cheap cable and then went to competitors to buy all of the other products they needed.

When they did the numbers the lost profit from this discounted price was definitely not being beaten, or even matched, by any additional profit generated from sales of other goods arising from these price promotions. There was certainly a higher footfall in the branch, but these customers were just taking advantage of the special deals and then moving on. This *loss leader* approach didn't work, and actually undermined the whole company price position as many customers got to know that which branch they shopped in would have a big impact on the price they paid. Customers hate unfairness!

The truth of the matter is that it is once again a crisis of confidence or lack of knowledge of the salespeople. Somewhere they have heard that supermarkets sell bread and milk as *loss leaders* to generate customer footfall into the store, and that these customers then spend loads more money on lots of other items. So they have adopted this approach themselves, without the financial evidence to back it up. The reality is that it is simply much easier to sell a product for *less* than it is to sell it for *more*. The branch manager didn't crunch the numbers to ensure that the strategy worked properly.

There are, however, a few situations where this approach can work, but it does require proper financial analysis to make sure that losing money on one product is justified by the profit that is made on another. What the business needs to do is to make the discounting of the first product to be conditional on the purchase of other products.

That is, the electrical wholesaler could have pushed the cut-price cable with a promotion that said:

- Cable at £20 for a 50 metre box *whenever you spend £200 or more* on other items – maximum three boxes per customer.

- 1 × 50 metre box of cable at £20 *whenever you buy a consumer unit at £50 or above*.

- Cable at £20 for a 50 metre box for all *account customers spending more than £1,000 per month*.

The special price is only available to those customers from whom you are certain that you will make something back from other sales or as a reward to loyal customers that are already spending a lot with you. Whatever your business, selling some products at very low prices in the *hope* that it is generating profits elsewhere is very unlikely to succeed.

Myth: A 50 per cent off sale is a 50 per cent off sale

Consider what is perhaps the biggest lie of all on pricing issues – the *50 per cent off sale*.

You will have seen many times on the TV, billboards and online, adverts for sofas, three-piece suites, kitchens, etc all offering massive discounts of 50 per cent off, or even higher at 70 per cent off the marked prices. These may be promoted as special *Bank holiday madness* or *Balmy summer sales* although we all know that most of these companies appear to have permanent sales.

How can these companies afford to give these massive discounts and still make a profit? Perhaps they are only promoting selected deals in the hope that this will bring customers into the store to buy other items at higher prices? Having just explored the fallacy of the idea of *loss leaders* above, and considering that these 50 per cent deals are usually across the whole range of products, it simply doesn't make any sense for them to be discounting prices as a way of generating profits from other product sales. Certainly the odds on buying a second three-piece suite or a second brand-new kitchen are slim to say the least.

The objective of the store is to promote a compelling message of exceptional value that gets customers to come and take a look. They make their side of the Value Scales higher by pretending that the items are worth more than they really are. The 50 per cent off sale is nothing more than a marketing hook to get your attention.

The reality is of course that the discount is nonsense. Let's look at a leather sofa from a typical high street retailer. The advert shows a special offer of 50 per cent off the list price of £1,000 reducing it to £500. Wow! A saving of £500 on what the customer would normally have been asked to pay for that sofa. A real bargain.

Look carefully at the advert or the small print on the promotional material and you will see something along these lines:

This item has been offered for sale at the full price for a period of at least 28 days in a UK store.

This narrative was brought in under the consumer protection legislation to stop companies simply plucking a price out of thin air in order to enable them to slash it with a fictitious discount offer. This prevents them from bluffing the customer into thinking that they have got a better deal than they actually have.

In the example, DFS worked out that they could buy a particular leather sofa for £300 from the manufacturer, and they would hope to sell it for £500 making a 40 per cent profit margin. They want to be able to promote it with a 50 per cent discount label, so they simply double the price to £1,000. They then stick it up for sale at this £1,000 price in the back of a store somewhere in the UK and bingo, 28 days later they can advertise it as 50 per cent off the list price. Whether they actually sold any at the higher price is doubtful, but in reality, irrelevant.

This practice happens all over the country in a number of different markets, particularly with those companies with multiple outlets and big advertising budgets. The truth is that there are no real discounts on these products, they are just capitalizing on the natural desire of consumers who want a bargain, and *pretending* that they can get a great deal.

Of course, from a business perspective, the big downside of these practices is that it is conditioning consumers to believe that the profit margins businesses make are huge, based on these high discounts that some businesses seem to be able to give away, and as a result we are seeing more and more customers expecting a discount on all sorts of purchases. A business that hasn't artificially inflated the price to start with must now overcome the customer's desire for these massive discounts either with better selling skills to explain why they can't give it (and all of the other good reasons to buy from them), or copy the other retailers and start with a made-up price from which they are then able to discount.

The question is whether the presentation of the price does have an impact on the customer's buying decision, or whether you are better off setting realistic prices in the first place and being prepared to defend against discount demands.

Myth: Presentation of the price doesn't matter

Consider the ways in which you can present the price of a new dress, and how this may influence a customer's decision to buy. The end result is that you want to actually get £100 into the till, so it isn't whether the actual price makes the difference, just how this is expressed and how this in turn affects the customer's perception of getting a great deal.

So how could you present the price of £100?

TABLE 8.3

Price presentation	Underlying message
The price is £100	Take it or leave it, that's the price
50 per cent off, now £100	Great deal, was £200, saved £100
Half-price sale, now £100	Great deal, was £200, saved £100
Special end-of-season price, £100	Worth more, but may be going out of fashion
Offer of the week only £100	Worth more, but time limit to deal
Now only £99.99	Special price – seems like a bargain
Was £150, you save £50	You are saving money by buying this item
£150 with £50 special cash back deal	Cash back deal may be removed if you delay
Our price is only £100	Implies competitors may be higher

Now, there are lots of ways of presenting a price, and you can see above that how you present it can have a profound effect on how it is perceived by the customer. Just consider for yourself which of these is most likely to persuade a customer to part with £100. Is it the clear no-frills factual statement number 1 that says *the price is £100* or is it option 2 or 3 where the perceived saving is greatest? The answer is that it depends on your customers; ie are they businesses or end consumers? It also depends on the product; ie is it a regular purchase or one-off occasional spend?

The critical point here is that presentation of a price can indeed have a profound impact on the customer's perception of the deal.

Chapter 10 explores in much greater depth the financial implications of discounting prices and why it simply doesn't work as a way of generating higher profits. It only works when it is used as a presentation tool to make the customer believe they have received a better deal than they actually have.

Myth: All prices should end in a '9'

You will see it everywhere you shop, whether clothes for £9.99 or £29.99, or even buying cars for £25,999. Although house prices rarely end in a 9, you can often see them promoted at, say, £399,995 for example.

So why is 9 such an important number?

Most people would suggest that there is some subtle psychology at work where £29.99 seems subconsciously good value, and it is in the £20s range of prices compared to just one penny more when it goes into the £30s range; ie one penny under a price threshold gives the customer a perception of good value. Maybe there is a little truth in that, as all of us will at some time have justified a frivolous purchase by saying something like *it was only twenty something pounds* or *it was under £30* when we have just blown £29.99 on something we didn't really need. But that is only a small part of the explanation.

So what is the true significance of 9?

If you are old enough to remember shopping in the early 1980s, you know that these were the days when we didn't buy everything on a debit or credit card, but instead we used either a chequebook or plain cash. Using cheques was a pain and as a result the vast majority of normal high street purchases were paid for by cash.

As well as being before the surge in credit and debit card payments, this was a time when very few retailers would allow you to return goods for a *no questions asked* refund if you decided it wasn't really what you wanted. Once you walked out of the shop, that's it, deal done. As a result, there simply wasn't the need to keep receipts for the purchase so that you could return that item a week later saying it was the wrong size or the wrong colour. If you are under 30 this may be hard to believe, but that's what it was like!

In this situation, imagine that a pair of jeans was on the rack priced at exactly £20. You are in a hurry, you have no need of a receipt because you have no option to return it later, and you have a £20 note in your hand. What happens at the till? Well what could happen is that you give the cashier your £20 note and simply walk away. If you did this, where could that £20 note go? It would either go straight into the till, or it could go straight into the cashier's pocket. Obviously the retailers tried to monitor this in a variety of ways, using mystery shoppers to test cashier honesty, and marked notes, etc, but it is a very difficult area to control properly. Therefore, to prevent this risk of cash theft, high street retailers priced every item at the highest price possible that would force the customer to wait for their change. Now the customer would hand over their £20 note and wait patiently for their 1p change. Even though this was an insignificant sum, customers would still stand and wait for change, forcing the cashier to ring the item through the till.

What this explains is that the prominence of 9 in the prices we now see on the high street is actually a result of decades of using prices ending in a 9 as a cash control mechanism, not some clever psychology of being below a key price threshold. We have all therefore become comfortable with the idea that prices should always end in a 9.

With the dominance of electronic payment methods, the importance of this as a cash control mechanism has now all but disappeared; however, customers have been indoctrinated into believing that a price with a 9 in it is to be expected, and that it is therefore likely to be the *right* price.

The real problem with this myth that setting prices just below key price breaks helps to encourage customers to buy, is that many businesses get stuck at prices just under a round sum amount and never get the courage to step over the threshold.

Chapter 11 explores in a lot more depth the significance of the actual numbers in pricing, but if you still work under the impression that setting a price at just below a round sum amount ending in a 9 is a critical psychological issue, then think again.

Myth: The best person to set the price is the salesperson

This is such a common statement spoken by salespeople; however, some others hold the view that the marketing team should set prices. But very rarely will you hear that it should be a decision for the finance department.

The justification for letting salespeople set prices is that they are closer to their customers, they know what their competitors are up to, and they need the flexibility to adjust the price at the point of sale to do the deal. This is perhaps a bit like letting the fox look after the chicken coop!

Setting prices is ultimately a financial decision. Any business needs to know what it costs to sell what they sell or do what they do. That includes understanding the hidden costs of running a business and how to properly allocate fixed costs across all of the things you sell. Even accountants can get embroiled in arguments about the best way to allocate overheads or absorb fixed costs. What is needed is a clear understanding of the financial impact of various pricing strategies. At a very simplistic level that may come down to a low price and high volume plan, or a high price and low volume one.

Armed with this information, the business then needs to understand what its competitors are up to, talk with its customers about what they want from each product or service, and a variety of other market research and investigation processes. Clearly the sales and marketing team are an essential part of the process.

Ultimately, price is a strategic decision for the business owners, CEOs, directors or managers to make. Where does the business want to fit in its marketplace? Does it want to be a premium price, high-quality business or a low-priced *value*-led organization, or even a *pile them high and sell them cheap* one? This should perhaps involve challenge and debate from all quarters to discuss the options, financial implications and the impact on the business's overall strategy for growth.

What is seen in most organizations is that there is little or no debate from any quarter, and in most cases it is the sales director or sales managers that have the greatest influence on what prices are charged. Even if there was some higher-level debate involving a wider group, this input is often wiped out by setting carefully thought out prices from which sales teams are then allowed to indiscriminately discount. Chapter 10 covers this in detail.

The problem with letting salespeople directly (or indirectly via uncontrolled discounts) set prices is twofold.

The first point is that they rarely have the financial skills to understand the implications of the decisions they make, and are not always directly accountable for them. Within a number of organizations with teams of salespeople, you will find countless examples where they have followed a course of action without any understanding of the financial implications. This isn't just the case with small businesses that lack any great sophistication on price, but happens in huge international organizations.

A number of online businesses have developed in recent years around the model of getting other suppliers to agree to give 40 per cent to 60 per cent discounts via *daily deals* to the online discount company's members. These are often hotels or restaurants, but cover a wide range of small- to medium-sized businesses. These suppliers are persuaded to give a discount in order to generate greater customer awareness and a surge of sales from the huge online membership of the discount company. Sadly, the failure rate of businesses that have run such promotions is quite high. This may be partly due to the fact that it is businesses already in difficulty that try these promotions, but research suggests that it is also because they have made no effort at all to quantify the impact of a huge surge in demand at much lower prices.

The fundamental problem was that no one had worked out the true costs of satisfying estimated or potential levels of demand that the promotion would create. If your restaurant is in trouble already, the last thing you need is to be inundated by customers who only pay half of the normal price. Whatever your idea for generating new business, there is a need to look at the costs of such a promotion, both directly in any advertising and sales efforts, and also in the impact of any price discounts, air miles, or free iPads, for example. If the benefit of increased sales of locked-in new customers doesn't match the investment then don't go ahead.

The second concern on letting salespeople set prices goes back to the tourist attraction example earlier. If we set prices based on our worst customers, we will inevitably set them lower in seeking to avoid the conflict of complaining customers. In the example, they wanted to drop prices for over 99,000 happy customers to avoid potential conflict with a very small minority that complained.

It is clear that the salespeople in any organization are the ones most likely to have had those bad experiences and therefore most likely to seek to consciously or subconsciously set prices low to avoid conflict in future. Therefore the suggestion that salespeople should determine prices as they are closer to the issues is exactly the reason why they should not be allowed to set the prices.

In every business the process should involve a group of people who all get to offer their input into the pricing debate, including the finance team, the sales team, and even perhaps the people involved in the delivery of the product or service. It then remains the decision of the business owners and CEOs to set the overall pricing strategy. Rarely however will you see this being the way it is done, and even when there is that level of sophistication and thought, it is wiped out by then allowing people on the frontline to give it all away with un-controlled discounting practices.

Myth: Setting prices is a once a year decision

In perhaps 99 per cent of businesses, the setting of prices is a once a year decision, although to call it a *decision* is to give it more importance than it actually receives within most businesses.

For those that do at least make some price changes, this is usually driven by a need to set prices for the season ahead (such as tourist attractions like DFAP, or other seasonal businesses for example) or a reflection of the habit they have simply got into of updating the price list in the same month each year. On the whole these businesses are not making any strategic adjustment, responding to market changes, or reflecting any revised assessment of the market value of what it is they are selling. It is just a mechanical price movement.

In an earlier chapter we explored the common ways in which prices are set, such as adding a fixed mark-up to cost price, or using last year's prices as the starting point for this year's, and any annual price adjustment doesn't cover any debate on whether the formula for determining the price is right. In most business we could see upwards of five years pass before there is any clear change in pricing policy.

There are many problems with the infrequency of the debate on prices. Like anything you do, the more often you do it, the better you become at it. If you do anything once a year, you will have forgotten most of the key issues that you debated the last time, and will be in effect starting all over again with raising skill levels and building knowledge. Furthermore, the prices that you set for the year ahead are completely tainted by the situation that prevails at the point of the review; ie if that is just after a month of low sales and complaining customers, you may set them too low, or if it follows a period of great sales figures and some exceptional new customers being won, you may be too bullish and set them too high. We all appreciate that a business has highs and lows during a year and setting prices annually makes it more likely that they won't be representative of your overall financial position.

In a really well-run business, pricing will be something that is on every board meeting agenda, and something that is openly debated and discussed on an ongoing basis. That may mean a revolving review of certain products each month, or looking at market sectors or particular groups of customers on a cyclical basis. The more natural we can make the discussion about prices, the less emotional we would be about the challenge of increasing them, or defending the issue with customers if questioned. Another point is made later in the book about the merits of *little and often* price increases where a business may add, say, just 0.5 per cent to prices in each of the four quarters of its financial year. Each individual price increase is insignificant when added, but at the end of the year prices are just over 2 per cent higher than they would have been. Many businesses can cope with justifying regular small increases but would struggle with a single larger one annually.

The problem for many businesses is that they have made price *the big issue*, and they often lack the courage to tackle the need to push prices forward and handle the fallout that 'may' result. By dealing with the issue on a regular basis, it simply becomes one of the issues that is discussed internally, raised with customers frequently, and any adverse reactions put properly into context.

If a business can make *price* simply another routine issue that requires attention, then a lot of the pressure or fear of the subject will disappear.

Any good business should have a process whereby they consider monthly, or at least quarterly, a range of business issues such as:

- current financial performance;
- marketing and business-generation issues;
- pipeline of orders;
- personnel matters (hire or fire / praise or reprimand);
- cash flow / banking issues;
- stock levels;
- product development or new lines to buy;
- pricing strategy and the changes needed to maximize profit.

Myth: Every customer is worth having and every sale matters

A large stationery and office equipment supplier was struggling with cashflow and at some risk of failure. The owner called in a consultant to talk with some of the senior team about the financial realities of the business and the actions that were needed.

One of the issues that cropped up, and which was causing a significant problem for the business, was the issue of incredibly low profit margins on some items. The sales manager was explaining why he believed it was OK to sell a ream of paper at £3.85, when it cost them around £3.75 to buy it. His argument was simply that every sale counts and that it was another £0.10 in the bag towards profits. He said that they sell a lot of paper and all those £0.10s add up. He didn't even argue that it was a loss leader, or that it led to happy customers buying other items, just that it was still a profit on every ream and that it all counts.

There is some logic to that attitude. They did sell a lot of paper, and they did make a £0.10 profit on each ream they sold.

The reality is that it simply wasn't worth the effort needed to just make £1 on a sale of 10 reams of paper. So the accountants looked at the underlying cost of the product. They needed to add something to the raw buying cost of £3.75 to reflect the fact that invoices needed to be raised for each sale as well as monthly statements for each account customer, debts had to be chased, and deliveries made. His defence was that for most customers they were already invoicing for something anyway, and delivering something, so that there was no real extra cost involved for the paper.

Like the loss leader example above, there were flaws in his logic, such as many cases where paper was indeed the only product that some customers bought (because it was so cheap!) so there really was a *cost to serve* of handling that sale to that customer. Probably the most interesting thing was that the amount of paper they bought in was quite significantly different from the amount they sold out. There were several reasons, and if your business handles stock you will no doubt come across them on a regular basis. There were always some boxes that were damaged a little. This meant that they were sold off cheap or occasionally simply thrown away. Reams of paper have no serial number, so are hard to track, hence quite a few went home in employees' briefcases for their home computers or kid's homework, etc. The final issue was the customer saying *if I buy twenty reams will you throw in one for free* to which sadly the response was most often *yes*. You don't need to be a mathematician to see that 20 reams at £0.10 each is only £2 of profit, which was completely wiped out by the cost (£3.75) of the one they threw into the deal.

The reality is that there are many occasions where the accumulations of all these small individual profits made is wiped out by one single event or action, and therefore actually not enough to reflect the real total costs of that deal; ie overall they lost money.

More importantly, he had missed a vital issue – *time*. The business probably sold over 100,000 reams of paper a year. That paper had to be checked in to stock. It had to be moved around, delivered to customers. Each sale needed an invoice even if they were doing a statement anyway for other items. Time costs money in the form of wages and National Insurance etc, but there is also a bigger cost – the opportunity cost of the time spent moving huge volumes of very-low-profit items that meant they were not spending that time looking after other customers and persuading them to buy more profitable products.

Look at a business that has a number of regular repeat clients or customers, such as commercial electricians or large printers for example.

If these businesses had accurate financial information to rank all of their customers based on the sales they generated, and if possible the profit they made from each one, they would undoubtedly see a wide range from the largest to the smallest. When you have the list, you can then draw a line at the point where it is probably uneconomic to do business, based on the administration costs of looking after the account, and perhaps simply the cost of taking on any customer in terms of opening credit accounts, setting up computer or physical files, sending out correspondence, etc.

Only you can decide where the line of *uneconomic to do business* is drawn. You could decide, for example, that any customer spending less than £1,000 a year isn't really profitable, or you could draw it at £50 a year, it doesn't initially matter. Wherever you draw the line there will always be a quite significant number of clients or customers that fall below it.

A survey of accounting practices asked these firms to list their clients by order of profitability from top to bottom. It was perhaps little surprise that the largest clients were generally (but not always) the most profitable, and the smallest generally (but not always) the least profitable, but what this survey found was that on average these accounting practices made 125 per cent of the firm's profits on the top 80 per cent of their clients, and actually lost 25 per cent of their profits (to be left with 100 per cent) on the bottom 20 per cent of clients.

A firm making a bottom line of £100k a year actually made £125k on the bulk of its clients, but lost £25k on the bottom end of the client list.

Ouch!

This situation is extremely common across a whole variety of industries and irrespective of the business's size. What is clear is that if the time and effort expended on the bottom 20 per cent of any business's customers was instead spent making sure that the top 20 per cent were given exceptional service, managed more proactively, and cultivated for referrals to similar businesses, etc, profit would increase dramatically.

Sometimes the profitable decision is to say *no* and turn down that sale or get rid of that small, difficult customer. Most salespeople would do a deal at anything above the raw cost, and often get suckered into doing deals where they either lose money, or they waste time that could be better spent elsewhere. Not every sale is worth having, and some customers are not as good as others. If you want to make more profit, learning to say *no* is a key issue.

Myth: Raising prices loses customers

This is, of course, one of the underlying themes of the book. If raising prices is matched with better explanation of value, or supported by quality guarantees, then many customers may well be prepared to pay more.

In many cases the right answer is to raise prices and accept that you will indeed lose some customers, but that overall you will make much more profit from the ones that stick than you will lose on the ones that leave. So raising prices and losing customers is OK, and in fact can be a really positive thing, by weeding out the low-value, price-sensitive, complaining customers that you lose money on anyway.

The myth is really that losing customers is an *inevitable* consequence of raising prices.

One of the features of a price is that it conveys to the customer a perception of value and quality simply by virtue of the amount. If you wanted to buy a watch, for example, you would be able to walk down any high street and see a range from just a few pounds to tens of thousands of pounds, and the perception of the average customer is that the more you spend the better the quality of the watch. So is there a real cost differential between a £4,000 Breitling and a £10,000 Rolex? Is there really a difference in the actual quality of the watches? Well, no doubt manufacturers would argue that there is, but in all probability the raw materials element and the manufacturing costs would not be significantly different. The main difference is in effect the *brand value*. This is the premium that any buyer pays based upon their perception of the value to them of the image that owning a Rolex will convey as opposed to a Breitling.

Therefore, increasing the price of certain products and services will change the perception of some customers about the underlying quality you will deliver.

One local business was struggling to make a profit. It didn't require much analysis to determine that they were simply not charging enough for the services they provided. For all of the reasons already explored in earlier chapters, they were petrified of the consequences of increasing their prices.

So it was suggested that a programme of calls to a sample of their clients should be undertaken, broadly like this:

> I wanted to call you personally as you are a valued and important client. We have been reviewing our business to ensure we are financially secure and will be able to continue to look after our customers properly over the coming years. The simple answer is that we don't believe we can do that at the low prices we are currently charging.
>
> It is therefore our intention to increase our prices over the next 12 months so that by then we will be 8 per cent more expensive than we are now. I wanted to let you know that in advance and to make sure you know that the reason for this is simply to enable us to maintain and improve the quality and standards of service that customers like you expect from us.
>
> I would hope that you would continue to do business with us, or at least let us know in advance any decision to leave. Can I count on your future custom?

Many of the responses were really positive, with some even saying that they were relieved with the decision, as they were keen to ensure that the supplier continued to look after them properly. There is a risk, of course, that many customers will say that they will stick around, and immediately go looking for an alternative. The situation was monitored, and six months later not a single customer had switched to another supplier.

The point is that many businesses selling top-quality items, whether jewellery, clothing, shoes, cars or holidays, use a high price to present a market position of high quality and exclusivity for their products. These businesses would not see any drop in sales if they increased their prices.

One final point is that prices can place a business into a particular consumer band, and that increasing the price can open up an entirely new group of customers. If you are trying to sell a house, you might place it on the market at say £299,000. Many potential customers may be setting their search criteria at £300,000 to £350,000 and wouldn't get your details from any search. Upping the price to say

£310,000, even if prepared to drop back down to the original price, will at least get you on their search list.

Summary

There are many myths that affect the way businesses and individuals set the prices they charge. These people have not taken an issue and decided to investigate the reality of it for their business or their products and services. They often take it at face value and set their prices based on this false perception.

All of these issues require attention, and for a group of people to debate and discuss all the key elements to the decision. If you leave the critical decision of pricing to your frontline team it will almost certainly result in profit being left on the table in many sales situations.

The true statements should be:

- Customers want value for money, not just the cheapest price.
- Loss leaders don't work.
- A 50 per cent off sale isn't really half price.
- Presentation of the price does matter.
- Prices shouldn't always end in a '9'.
- The salesperson is not the best person to set the price.
- Setting prices isn't just a once a year decision.
- Not every customer is worth having and not every sale matters.
- Raising prices might lose some customers, but that's OK.

Action points

Get your pricing team to review all of the myths covered above and how they may be an issue for your business. In particular:

1 Review all of your prices to ensure that there are no intentional or accidental loss leaders; ie that every product or service is priced to achieve an acceptable margin.

2 Review the way that your prices are expressed in all published locations (ie in sales literature, on your website, etc). Consider the options for representing these in a more dynamic way, such as using the expression *special prices*, or how you can uplift the core price to present a larger discount. Develop a plan to test these changes across a small number of products to measure the reaction of customers.

3 Ensure that the pricing team meet at least quarterly to debate and consider changes to prices regularly. Set the meeting dates for the next four meetings to ensure they are in diaries and properly prepared for.

4 Get the finance people in your pricing team to determine the point below which it is uneconomic to do business. This would take into account the effort needed to manage even the smallest customer and the profit that you need to make for an account to be worthwhile.

5 Produce a list of all the customers that are below the level set at point 4 and decide on appropriate action for each one, ranging from simply telling them you no longer wish to do business with them, to increasing the prices (or reducing any discounts they get) or holding an open and direct conversation to explain the financial realities.

Using guarantees to get increased prices

Earlier chapters covered variations of the critical issue in any buying decision, which is that customers take a risk when they buy. As the supplier, you also take some risk; for example as to whether you will get paid after the event, or in holding stock and materials that may never get used. Throughout this chapter you will see risk from each other's perspective.

The level of buyer risk varies depending on the specifics of the sale. At one end of the scale the risk is the concern of whether the supplier will actually deliver what was promised, when it was promised, and whether the price will be what the salespeople stated. As an example, a builder doing a kitchen extension that runs over budget and beyond the deadline.

At the simpler end of the scale is the risk for the buyer that they could have bought the same thing for a lower price by simply shopping around a little.

This chapter includes:

- Risk versus reward.
- Price-match guarantees.
- Using guarantees to add value.
- Offering options.
- Customers are fundamentally honest.
- Guarantees as an extra.

Risk versus reward

Every buying decision is a balance between risk and reward for the consumer. The reward is good value for money and the risk is that they overpay. The extremes are that the customer pays more than they should have, right up to a situation where the product or service delivered was unexpectedly different either in the final price or in substandard quality. Within these two extremes are, of course, many other variations of risk, such as quality not being as expected, delivery not on time, or service not quite up to standard. The consequences of these risks vary from real tangible loss, such as the kitchen extension falling down, to a simple disappointment that the customer could have got a better deal if they had tried a little harder.

It is the perception of risk that often holds up the decision to buy, as the customer is evaluating the balance between further shopping around and further negotiation to reduce the risk, versus the quick decision to take the deal on the table that may not be the best one.

Now add *price* into the equation.

Just think for a moment about how much time and research you would put into a buying decision to spend £50,000 on an extension to your home. You would almost certainly try to find a builder who had worked for someone you know who could comment on the quality of their work. You will probably go into a little bit of detail about the exact standard of finishes such as door handles, light fittings, etc. You would certainly talk about timescales and payment terms. This is all understandable as £50,000 is a lot of money, and there are many things to possibly go wrong.

Compare that with the decision to buy a kettle for the office kitchen. Whether you bought it at full retail price or at a sale price, the reality is that it is a small amount of money. You cannot know how good it will be when you buy it, although you may rely on a brand value, but most kettles are pretty similar and do the same job. The point is that the decision involved a comparatively small amount of money, a lower risk, and is therefore easier to make.

What this shows, and what you know instinctively, is that the higher the price the more thought goes into the purchase. However, for all customers the relationship between higher price and higher risk is clear. It is also generally true that higher priced items tend to be more complex purchases; ie a £400,000 house comes with many elements to the decision-making, such as location, school catchment, proximity of neighbours, etc. A £10 decision on a pair of trousers is as simple as 'will they fit and do they look OK?'

If you want to command higher prices for what you do, then you are likely to be moving the decision further up the risk scale for the customer. Let's say that you are looking for somewhere to eat. You find two restaurants that both look OK, but one has starters for £3 each and main courses for £12 each, while the other has starters for £4 and mains for £16.

Both are generally at the end of the scale where your risk is low as you will probably spend around £50 for two people, which is at a level which doesn't cause you to debate at length whether you can afford to eat out. However, the more expensive restaurant looks like being about one third more expensive than the alternative and you as the customer are being asked to take a risk that it is at least one third better. *Better* is a subjective issue: nicer ambience, better food choices, higher standard of service, higher quality ingredients, etc. Subconsciously you are being asked to consider 'will it be worth the extra £s that I am being asked to pay?'

In some way, every customer on every purchase is being asked to take a risk that the product or service that they are committing to buy will be worth the amount they are being asked to pay. Any doubt at all usually leads to either further shopping around – hence a risk for the seller that they may buy elsewhere – or be a simple *no sale*.

So what can businesses do to reduce the *perception* of risk for the customer and increase both the chances of a sale and the opportunity to charge a higher price?

The answer is to actually reduce the risk.

Price-match guarantees

Many businesses offer a guarantee that if you see the same product from another supplier for less money, then they will match that price or even beat it. Most of the large supermarkets currently offer some form of price-match guarantee.

ASDA's guarantee is: *If we're not 10 per cent cheaper than Tesco, Sainsbury's, Morrisons and Waitrose on your comparable grocery shopping we'll give you the difference. Guaranteed!*

Tesco offers: *We'll give you a voucher for the difference if your comparable grocery shopping is cheaper at ASDA, Sainsbury's or Morrisons.*

So why do the big supermarkets do this, and does it work?

They know that customers are able to switch supermarkets easily and that shoppers generally are looking for a nice place to shop that offers them value for money (but not necessarily the lowest prices). Therefore to remove the supermarket's risk that customers will shop around for cheaper prices and as a result buy elsewhere, they make a promise that they have already done this exercise and are already offering the best value for money. The confidence with which they promote their prices is enough in itself for the vast majority of their customers to stick with their usual supermarket.

But how can they all be the cheapest? They answer is, of course, that they are not. Each business's guarantee has a set of conditions that apply, such as which products are included within the price-matched range, and how this is compared with the other supermarkets, a minimum number of items to be purchased, etc. There are detailed examples of products that cannot be compared, and conditions and limitations on how often the customers can claim, etc. It is practically impossible to get any indication from any major supermarket as to how many items are available to check as part of their price guarantee, although all of them have quite long lists of whole areas of their business that are excluded from the comparison process.

Is it a trick? No, all of these supermarkets will clearly honour any guarantee they offer. The point is that very few people actually bother to make the price comparisons, and even fewer then claim for the vouchers or rebates they are entitled to. They rely instead on the general assumption that by promising to refund the difference the supermarket has already checked and is offering lower prices as a result. Even if customers do claim under the guarantee, the retailer fulfils the guarantee by giving vouchers that bring that customer right back into their store.

In the next chapter we explore the general concept of discounts and make the point that by lowering all of your prices you end up giving discounts to say 90 per cent of your customers who didn't ask for it, because of the 10 per cent who do. A relatively small proportion of customers are actually that sensitive on price. This equates exactly to the price guarantees. By offering to lower prices on a relatively small range of comparable products, it is satisfying those price-sensitive customers who bother to check and claim any refund, but not actually reducing the prices to the rest of us who cannot be bothered. They only give the discount to the 10 per cent who bother to check and ask for it.

So why do these supermarkets all offer price-match guarantee? Quite simply it's because everyone else does it. They cannot be seen to send a message that would be interpreted as *we know we are more expensive, but we don't care.*

Using guarantees to add value to your side of the Value Scales

In the context of your own business, guarantees help to overcome most customers' fear of the general buying risk, by removing one aspect of the risk they perceive they are taking. At the most basic level the perception of buyers' risk is that there may be a cheaper price just around the corner; ie a price-match guarantee. At the most complex level it is a complete guarantee of satisfaction, with an all-encompassing statement of *if you're not 100 per cent happy we offer a 100 per cent no-questions-asked refund.*

However, the most crucial aspect to understand is that if you set the guarantee, *you set the rules.* All of the supermarkets have a long list of rules governing when their price-match guarantee applies and to which products, and ASDA even prevent you checking for a period of time (supposedly to allow computers to update) which often means people simply don't check.

From a pricing perspective, offering any levels of reassurance adds value to your proposition, especially if it is something that is not available from your potential competitors. Putting more value on your side of the Value Scales increases the odds of a deal being done.

A business consultancy runs projects for various organizations that cover many aspects of business efficiency. Essentially what is promised is an improvement in bottom line profits if the business follows the advice.

The problem for the consultant, and for their clients, is that it isn't really clear exactly how those improvements will be delivered when a project is started. Often these clients are struggling, and therefore the potential cost of external involvement is a big step and a big risk. If the price is a take-it-or-leave-it option based simply on the time estimated to do the work, payable regardless of success, would any customer be willing to take that risk?

Offering options with and without guarantees

Consider three choices offered to the client as the basis for engagement on a project to drive their business forward and its profits up.

---

1 Buyer's Risk: a fixed price of £20,000 (payable by client regardless of the success of the project).

2 Seller's Risk: a 100 per cent guaranteed fee of £30,000 (only paid if client believes it was worth it).

3 Shared Risk: a hybrid fee with £7,500 fixed payment upfront, and a success element of between £7,500 and £17,500 ie a maximum of £25,000 (success fee at client's discretion).

Which you would choose?

Option 1 means that regardless of the outcome of the work, the business has to pay the £20,000 fee. Clearly, many smaller businesses would have no experience of paying professionals in any area of their business this kind of sum, and it would be a really big decision to make. Add to that the inherent uncertainty as to whether it would deliver results higher than the cost, and that the business owner would have no great understanding of what the consultant would even do during the project, and you can see how hard it might be to close the sale on this basis.

Option 2 allows the business to decide, *after* the event, whether they believe the project has added value sufficient to warrant the £30,000 fee. Although the consultant would help set the objectives of the project – that it should add directly to profits of at least the amount of the fee in year one – the guarantee is that the assessment of value is for the client to determine on any basis they see fit. They can pay any amount between £0 and £30,000.

Option 3 shares the risk between the buyer and seller so that the seller will earn at least £7,500 to cover basic set-up costs and some of his time, but with a total overall cost at £25,000, if the buyer accepts the value has been added.

What did you select? Assuming that you felt the need to do something to drive your business forward, would you consider option 1 at all, and if so would you rather pay a premium of 50 per cent to get the 100 per cent no-risk guarantee of value? Or would you choose the hybrid of shared risk?

Now consider it from the consultant's perspective. Can they afford to give an absolute no-questions-asked guarantee over £30,000 worth of work? Won't clients take this option and simply use the guarantee to avoid paying?

Look at the maths on options 1 and 2. The consultant will essentially do the same amount of work to deliver the project irrespective of the payment option selected. They will expect to make a profit even on the £20,000 option because the hourly rates used to budget for the project are designed to cover wage costs, overheads and a contribution to overall profits. Say it will cost £15,000 to do the work leaving £5,000 as the profit on this option. If the client chooses the guaranteed option 2 (£30,000), the consultant will therefore make a £15,000 profit providing the client decides that they have delivered the desired results. This premium (an extra £10,000) reflects the Seller's Risk that they have taken of not getting paid at all.

In other words, if only half the projects where the full guarantee is offered go to plan, then the consultant will at least cover the costs of doing the work on all of them (2 × £15,000 costs and 1 × £30,000 fee collected). If two out of every three pay up, then the consultant will make the same profit as if all three had chosen the cheaper fixed price option (3 × £15,000 costs and 2 × £30,000 fee, leaves £15,000 profit, equal to 3 × £5,000 profit on the fixed price option).

The decision for the customer is easy. The lowest price is £20,000 but they take all the risk, and £30,000 is the highest price but the consultant takes all the risk. For the consultant the decision is a combination of:

- Does the consultant believe they can deliver profit improvements in excess of the £30,000 fee?

- Does the consultant trust the client to pay a fair fee if they do deliver results?

- Can the consultant afford to cover the costs of doing the work if they don't get paid?

Customers are fundamentally honest

Think for a moment about human nature.

As covered in previous chapters, if a business offers three choices, that alone will increase their chances that the customer will choose one of them. People inherently avoid risk, and in the above example the customer has been offered one option where they have no risk at all. They are completely in control of the assessment of value and hence the level of fee.

The Seller's Risk option allows for customer discretion to pay between £0 and £30,000. Even if a project has not run perfectly to plan, very few clients would assess the contribution at £0, and if they agree to *meet halfway* the consultant has at least covered the costs of the project.

Most people in business are fundamentally honest. They are fair and reasonable in their assessment of the value of the work consultants do.

The consultancy firm offering these guarantees is therefore able to charge an overall premium on the standard fixed fee of around 40 per cent, being a mix of some clients choosing the full guarantee Seller's Risk Option 2 and some of the Shared Risk Option 3. This is simply because the consultant assumes most of the risk of delivering improvements in the bottom line profit.

This principle can be applied across almost any business and almost any product and service. That is, your chances of making a sale increase the more of the buying risk you take on. That may be as simple as the promise that you are comparable in price with the nearest alternatives (like the supermarket price-match), or as challenging as an absolute *no-questions-asked* refund guarantee. Not only are the chances of making a sale greater, but the reality is that only a small percentage of customers will invoke any guarantee offered.

If this risk reduction for the customer is reflected in a higher price for the product or service, then overall the business's profitability will increase. What you cannot do is to offer guarantees without that being reflected in the price. You can, of course, choose to offer only one option, which comes with the guarantee, or you may decide to offer the choice between a *take-it-or-leave-it deal* at one price and a *guaranteed* one at another.

Offering a guarantee as an extra

One variation further is what you will see in most electronic goods retailers, which is a price including only the statutory guarantees of quality (ie a 12-month warranty) with an additional charge to increase this to a 5-year warranty. Can this work in other businesses?

A holiday lettings business added a premium of £100 to the price of every week's booking in their homes during the summer. This was matched with the *Guaranteed Summer Sun* deal whereby they offered a rebate of £100 to cover the cost of indoor activities if it happened to rain for more than half the holiday.

Restaurants may guarantee a speedy lunchtime service with a *free meal* if not delivered to the table within 20 minutes of the time of the order.

Most retailers now offer a refund policy well in excess of their statutory obligations because they know that this encourages customers to spend more in the knowledge that it can simply be returned if they change their mind. Many years ago when returns policies were only offered in the event of a fault with the product, Marks & Spencer stood out from their competition by offering a simple refund or exchange policy, even though it was with M&S vouchers. Many of their customers chose to shop there simply because they had the confidence that they could return anything they wanted, and M&S were able to charge a premium price for their products in part because customers valued this reassurance.

These days most retailers offer this returns policy, because research tells them that knowing they can return items if needed encourages many customers to buy more than they otherwise would (particularly clothing items, for example) and that many of these customers simply don't bother to return items anyway. Even if they do return items, the odds are that much of the amount to be refunded will then be immediately spent on other purchases in their store.

If you look hard enough at your business, there will be a number of ways in which you can express your willingness to remove some of the risk that the customer takes when they make a decision to buy from you. That is absolutely a key part of the selling process, but it must also be coupled with a premium, however small, on the prices you charge. If you offer added value that has a potential cost to you, and fail to reflect this in the price, you will not only make less profit but also risk your own business.

One business explored this issue and started to look at all the things that they might be able to guarantee. This included replacing faulty goods, swapping the item if it was unsuitable even if it was the customer's mistake, speed of delivery to the customer, price matching, etc.

As they talked through these issues as a group, they found that many of the frontline people responded with comments like, 'We already do swaps for customers if they bought the wrong item – that's just good service – we already tell customers that goods will always be delivered same day if ordered before lunchtime and next day if not', and even 'If they came back and complained that they found an item at a competitor's for less, we usually give them a credit note for the difference anyway.'

There were many more examples of value-added reassurances for customers that came out of a number of these sessions. In other words, they were already offering really high standards of guarantee, but there were three significant issues:

- They were not expressing these points anywhere for existing or, more importantly, potential customers to see.

- The informality of the approach meant that it was inconsistently applied across the business and across the customers.

- It was not being reflected in their prices.

Overall, the business was offering a far lower level of buying risk to its customers, albeit inconsistently, while price matching with competitors that did not offer these same reassurances.

Ouch!

They subsequently spent time clarifying what guarantees the business should be offering and to what limits, and then ensuring that this was applied consistently across the business, properly expressed and that prices reflected that level of protection provided to the customer.

A side effect of this clarity was that the occasionally difficult customer who simply wanted a rock-bottom price could be offered a special deal, but without all of the guarantees that other customers got; ie *you can have it for 15 per cent less, but you must collect it and you will not be able to return it for any reason at all.*

Summary

Customers are significantly more likely to buy if there is a guarantee that removes some or all of their buying risk, and as a result they are also more likely to pay a premium price for that piece of mind.

Guarantees can take many forms, from the vague and simple *guaranteed service with a smile* to the extreme and explicit *100 per cent no-questions-asked money-back guarantee*.

The key is that when you set the guarantee, you call the shots. You decide what is covered and what is not. You decide what premium is paid for the peace of mind that the guarantee offers, and you set all the terms and conditions that apply.

Action points

1 Get your pricing team to look at all the things you currently offer to customers as *peace of mind* or *quality assurances*. Look at how you can express these better to be seen as *guarantees* for which a price premium can be added, and ask them to make recommendations for change.

2 Look at all of your products and services and consider the risk that the customer takes when they buy from you.

- On-time delivery. Not having your product or service in time may have a critical consequence for the customer.

- Quality. If the product or service fails in some way, what would be the knock-on impact for them? For example, inconvenience if the service is just slow, or potentially life-threatening if the brake pads you sell fail.

- Value for money. How can you reassure the customer that your prices are *fair*? Can you present price comparisons for them, offer a refund of the difference, or simply say *we have set our prices to reflect the fair price for the quality and service we deliver*.

- A change of mind. Can you encourage a quick decision by removing the risk that it is irrevocable? For instance, *seven days to change your mind for a full refund*.

There are many more, and asking some trusted and valued customers, and even some lost customers, may be very useful.

Ask them to tell you what you could offer to reduce their perception of buying risk.

3 Now look at all the things you unconsciously guarantee anyway. What would you do if a customer said, 'Sorry, I made a mistake and bought the wrong item', or 'I changed my mind and I don't want this anymore', or 'Joe Bloggs down the road was actually £10 cheaper, what are you going to do about it?'

Get your sales team involved and find out what they already do in these situations, or what they would probably do if they arose.

Armed with this information, develop a list of 5 to 10 things you could expressly guarantee as a way of differentiating yourself from your competitors and as a way of charging a premium price for some of them.

Shortlist this to three guarantees that attract a premium price and test it with some customers. Then update procedures and training materials, and retrain your people so that these things become part of the new way of doing business.

4 For all of the changes you propose, make sure your finance people run the numbers to ensure that the guarantee is affordable for you and matched properly with a premium price adjustment. Get them to monitor the financial impact based on how many customers choose the guaranteed option versus the number that claim on the guarantee.

10 Discounting

Pressure on price leads many businesses into discounting. It is this practice which has the greatest negative impact on the profits achieved by the vast majority of business. Getting a grip on discounts could be critical to your own future success.

The key is that if your business gives discounts then this chapter could well be the most important in the whole book. Before getting into some of the reasons or remedies for this massive problem, it will be helpful to understand the financial dynamics.

Although it may well be impossible to eradicate discounting from your business, simply scoring the cost accurately, training your people to understand the implications, and putting in place basic disciplines to control it, will have a profound impact on your bottom line.

In this chapter you will learn:

- Who is affected by poor discounting practices.
- The financial dynamics of discounting.
- The impact of a small change in discounts.
- Discounting prices to win customers is a myth.
- Top four reasons why people discount.
- How to limit discounts.

Who is affected by poor discounting practices

Most businesses now operate in an environment where discounts are expected – even *demanded* – by customers, but some are more affected than others.

If you run a traditional *business-to-business* (B2B) operation then you will almost certainly discount your prices to some customers, at some time, and on some products. Many of you will have institutionalized discounting practices across all customers, all products and at all times.

You may be a retail business dealing with the end consumer and many of these businesses don't have such a great problem. When we walk into a major retail store, such as a DIY warehouse, we see marked prices and mostly accept them as non-negotiable. Rarely do people get to the till and ask the cashier to *knock a bit off*. Certainly pubs, restaurants and such businesses rarely get challenges on their prices. It is simply a *take-it-or-leave-it* approach. But haggling even in these businesses is becoming more common, and especially in independent retailers where the customer feels that there may be some flexibility as prices have not been *fixed* by 'head office'.

The financial dynamics of discounting

CASE STUDY

Special Events Limited (SE Limited) was a long-established large business, selling and hiring out specialist equipment to a mix of businesses and end consumers. Their turnover was £25m a year. Times had been getting tough in this very capital-intensive business, and they were not generating sufficient profit to continue investing in their future.

So, like many businesses they started a two-pronged attack through: a) marketing to win new business; and b) initiating a cost-cutting programme.

Broadly their numbers looked like Figure 10.1 on the following page.

The owner asked for external help with a cost-cutting programme, which of course always begins with examining the biggest costs.

Spending £18m on products to sell leaves some room for negotiation with suppliers, even with a good in-house buying team. Payroll is tougher, as cuts are hard to implement, and have an immediate cost of redundancy and negative impact on morale. Operating costs could be reduced by shopping around or cutting back, but on areas like *sales and marketing* this conflicts with the other objective of driving up sales. Many businesses can shave perhaps 10 per cent

FIGURE 10.1

special events
LIMITED

PROFIT AND LOSS ACCOUNT
FOR THE YEAR ENDED 31 DECEMBER

	£,000's	£,000's
Turnover		£25,000
Opening stock	£3,000	
Purchases in the year	£19,000	
	£22,000	
Closing stock	£(4,000)	
Cost of goods sold		£18,000
Gross profit	28%	£7,000
Overheads		
Payroll	£4,000	
Property costs	£800	
Sales and marketing expenses	£600	
Finance costs	£350	
Distribution costs	£300	
Other overheads	£200	
Total overheads		£6,250
Net profit before tax		£750

off their costs with a little effort, putting contracts out to tender, or gently haggling with existing suppliers.

Sadly, business owners and managers often miss one cost altogether, and it is a big one – one which most people don't control. For SE Limited that could have been worth more than £5m a year.

A *discount* is the difference between the price that you hoped to get and the amount you actually achieve after you have been haggled down by arguments about how much they are spending with you and with the veiled threat to go elsewhere.

In SE Limited, they were able to accurately calculate the average discount given on all products for all customers at 21 per cent. This was no surprise to the CEO, and in fact he thought it might actually be even higher. But he still wasn't quite sure how this debate related to a review of costs.

The impact of discounting can be illustrated by producing a new profit and loss account with some extra numbers:

FIGURE 10.2

special events
LIMITED

PROFIT AND LOSS ACCOUNT
FOR THE YEAR ENDED 31 DECEMBER

	£,000's	£,000's
Full value turnover		£31,650
Discounts given	21%	£6,650
Actual invoiced turnover		£25,000
Opening stock	£3,000	
Purchases in the year	£19,000	
	£22,000	
Closing stock	£(4,000)	
Cost of goods sold		£18,000
Gross profit	28%	£7,000
Overheads		
Payroll	£4,000	
Property costs	£800	
Sales and marketing expenses	£600	
Finance costs	£350	
Distribution costs	£300	
Other overheads	£200	
Total overheads		£6,250
Net profit before tax		£750

If the turnover figure reported in the accounts was £25m – *after* an average 21 per cent discount – then the turnover *before* the discount would have been £31.65m and that meant discounts given away added up to £6.65m. Sadly, in almost all businesses, the money lost by uncontrolled discounting is not reported in the financial statement and nor in management accounts. The starting point for every sales transaction is the amount *actually charged*.

It may not be possible to wipe out this cost, in much the same way as it would be impossible to reduce payroll to zero. However, in the case of SE Limited, it is the second biggest cost after the cost of the goods bought for resale and way above the hard-to-reduce payroll bill.

The impact of a small change in discounts

Consider the impact of reducing this business cost by a small amount. If we aim to reduce the overall cost of the discounts given by say 5 per cent, this would in effect be a reduction of 1.05 per cent in the overall discount rate (5 per cent of 21 is 1.05), reducing it from 21 per cent to an overall average of 19.95 per cent.

First, what would this look like from the customer's side of the deal?

- A customer who previously bought a £220 switching control box only paid £173.80 after 21 per cent discount; ie £46.20 profit was given away.

- If the business reduced the discount to the new 19.95 per cent level, the price paid would become £176.11, and the discount would reduce to £43.89.

- The customer therefore only pays an extra £2.31 above the old price of £173.80, equivalent to an overall price increase of just 1.3 per cent.

Now, would you expect any customers to walk away from something that is just £2.31 – 1.3 per cent – more expensive? Or based on a conversation that says, *Sure we can give you a discount, it's 19.95 per cent* (rather than 21 per cent) *off list price, if that's OK?* It is unlikely that this change would even be noticed by the majority of customers.

From the business's side, what would be the impact if they cut back on discounts from the average of 21 per cent to 19.95 per cent (a 5 per cent drop) by being a little bit more sophisticated in their sales pitch, or just a little more disciplined in the way discounts are offered? What would it mean to the business overall?

- Getting the discount bill of £6,650,000 down by 5 per cent would release a staggering £332,500, which would filter down to net profit (as all other costs are unchanged).

- Profit was just £750,000, so this increases profits from £750,000 to £1,083,500 – a 44.3 per cent increase!

- In fact every 1 per cent drop in discounts is a £66,500 saving, equivalent to a price increase of 0.27 per cent (27p on a £100 item) but increases profits by 8.9 per cent.

This is easily achievable, and indeed the impact can be very much more. The effect on businesses is seeing their gross profit margins increase dramatically through simply managing discounts more actively.

You may be thinking that these numbers are simply irrelevant to your scale of business. Whatever the size of your operation, you will almost certainly find that discounts represents one of your top three business costs, up there with the cost of whatever you buy to sell and the payroll. Whatever the amount of money you *give away*, clearly some attention to it will help you reduce that cost. Every £1 you shave off discounts is £1 straight to your bottom line profit.

The critical starting point is to quantify it. This follows the maxim:

What you can measure, you can manage.

What you manage, you can improve!

Discounting can be looked at from a slightly different perspective, which reinforces its importance.

Discounting prices to win customers is a myth

Many business people, and in particular those working on the front-line of sales, would argue that they *need* to give discounts or they will lose customers, or that they couldn't win that new customer without the ability to discount the price. I would argue that better selling skills is the right answer, but let's assume they are right. The question is of course, are they giving away more money in the *value* of discounts offered than they are getting back in increased profits from extra sales to existing customers, or in sales won from new customers?

Figure 10.3 shows across the top various gross profit margins from 20 per cent to 60 per cent. Down the column on the left are proposed price discounts from 2 per cent to 20 per cent that could be used to try and increase sales. The results in the middle are the extra volume of sales that a business needs to achieve in order to replace the profit lost by dropping the price. Now this may be applied to your business as a whole, at whatever your average profit margin is, or you could do the exercise on a product-by-product basis. The calculations are exactly the same.

Simply find the column with the correct gross profit margin for your business or the product under review, and then look at the line across that represents the discount you are considering giving to boost the volume of sales.

For example:

The sales manager of a business that sells digital photo frames says: *I want to drop our prices by 10 per cent so that I can increase our sales.* The business currently buys the frames for £70, sells them for £100, and is therefore making a £30 or 30 per cent gross profit margin. They sell 1,000 frames a year at £100 each so have turnover of £100k, costs of £70k, and £30k or 30 per cent gross margin.

FIGURE 10.3

The effect of discounting on sales volumes

Your current gross profit margin

GP%	20%	25%	30%	35%	40%	45%	50%	55%	60%

To produce the same profit, you must increase your sales volumes by...

Proposed price discounts									
2%	11%	9%	7%	6%	5%	5%	4%	4%	3%
4%	25%	19%	15%	13%	11%	10%	9%	8%	7%
6%	43%	32%	25%	6%	5%	5%	4%	4%	4%
8%	67%	47%	36%	30%	25%	22%	19%	17%	15%
10%	100%	67%	50%	40%	33%	29%	25%	22%	20%
12%	150%	92%	67%	52%	43%	36%	32%	28%	25%
14%	233%	127%	88%	67%	54%	45%	39%	34%	30%
16%	400%	178%	114%	84%	67%	55%	47%	41%	36%
18%	900%	257%	150%	106%	82%	67%	56%	49%	43%
20%	*	400%	200%	133%	100%	80%	67%	57%	50%

If they cut their prices by 10 per cent, and sell the next 1,000 for only £90 then the turnover reduces to £90k. However, the purchase cost of these 1,000 items remains the same at £70k and the gross profit therefore drops to only £20k. Unless volumes do increase they have just lost £10k.

At the new £90 selling price they now make only £20 profit after the £70 costs. So to recover the lost £10k of profit they need to sell 500 more units, just to get back to where they were.

If your margin was only 20 per cent and you discounted by 10 per cent to drum up new sales, then you would need to *double* your volumes to get back to where you started. The stark reality is that if you are discounting prices in the belief that it will stimulate additional volumes of business that more than make up for the lower profit margins, then quite simply you can't.

There are only two valid reasons for discounting. First, where you are using it as a marketing tool to present the price in an attractive way, and have set your initial prices to be able to do this. (Re-read the section in Chapter 8 exploding the myth 'A 50 per cent off sale is a 50 per cent off sale'.) Second, when your prices are wrong and need to be adjusted to the real market value. Before you use this reason you need to have done some serious market research to get your facts straight.

So why does everyone discount?

The top four reasons people discount

1 Because everyone else does it

Discounting in the business-to-business marketplace is following that of the retail marketplace. We have all become conditioned to the fact that when we walk into a supermarket or an electrical retailer, we will be greeted by signs offering:

- buy one, get one free;
- sale – 20 per cent off marked items;
- 50 per cent off selected end-of-season goods;
- spend over £50 and get an extra 10 per cent off these items.

There are many different permutations of these examples, but they all essentially offer a discount to customers. What that has done is to condition us to believe that there is opportunity to knock the price down a bit where we have been given a *full* or *list* price only.

Whatever the offer in the shop, we accept completely the new stated price. If the sign says that the price was £100, and is now £80 we accept this as being non-negotiable. However, if we were told by a business supplier that the price was £100, and we have discounted it to £80 many customers would still ask for a further discount. What this demonstrates is that the act of asking for discount is not actually a desire to try and get the Value Scales to balance because we genuinely value the item at less than the supplier has asked for.

It is not a real concern with the actual price, but just an automatically conditioned response to the price offered. When changes are made to teach frontline people how to politely say *No* when asked for a discount, the most common response from their customers has been *Oh well, worth a try*!

Inevitably, decades of price-driven marketing has meant that discounting has become a business way of life, and failure to offer one is seen like an attempt to overcharge or rip off the customer. Obviously if everyone does it, it is going to be hard for you in your business to stand alone and refuse to offer discounts. What we need to do is find a more subtle way of managing the problem. There are a good number of techniques later in the chapter.

One company really took the point, publishing a Discount Policy as part of its terms of trade. This notice was included with every quote and added to the footers of company emails.

DISCOUNT POLICY

As a company we work very hard to ensure that we can provide our customers with the highest quality goods, exceptional customer service, and at real value for money.

Our prices have all been determined after great consideration, at a level to enable us to achieve these things, and to make a fair profit.

Further discounts on our prices could only be achieved at the expense of reducing the quality of our products, or our standards of service, neither of which we are prepared to do.

So please do not ask for a discount, as the prices we offer are already the very best we can do.

They actually found they won business through this absolutely transparent pricing model, and certainly made a lot more profit by removing the random, uncontrolled discounting practices of their past.

2 Because they think it will increase sales volumes

We have commented already about the fallacy of this argument. Figure 10.3 showed for various gross profit margins, the additional business that is needed to replace the profit lost by a number of different price reductions.

> The possibility of volume increases being sufficient to replace the profit given away is almost always nil.

It is important to explain, however, that seeking to increase volumes by dropping prices *is* a reason why many businesses do discount. This is as a result of not understanding the financial dynamics that are so visible in the earlier grids. They aren't using carefully calculated figures, or basing decisions on detailed analysis of customer reaction. They just see all the big retailers running regular price offers, and think that these huge businesses must have done their homework and determined that discounting prices will generate extra sales and extra profits. What they fail to understand is that the retailers' motivation to discount is for completely different reasons.

Look at a retailer selling a typical women's jacket. They placed 1,000 units in the local outlet, selling at £49. At a cost of £29.40, they make 40 per cent (or £19.60) gross profit on each one. They sell 800 jackets at this price, over the first three months.

They are then faced with 200 items left to sell, and the new season's lines coming in very soon. So they reduce the price by 20 per cent to £39. They now only make £9.60 on each item, roughly half the profit they did at the original price. This would not be an economic profit level on the whole 1,000 items of stock, but having already made a good profit on the 800 they sold, their motivation has now changed to one of clearing the shelves at the best deal they can, and not of generating overall profit.

Sales and profit results:

800 units × £19.60 profit margin = £15,680 profit.

So even if they throw away the remaining 200 items, they are still ahead:

200 units × £29.40 cost = £5,880 loss.

Profit on first 800 units	£15,680
Loss on 200 thrown away	£(5,880)
Overall profit on all 1,000 units	£9,800

If they can clear the last 200 units at their cost of £29.40, then the overall profit jumps back to £15,680. Anything above cost, then they are more than happy with the overall result. In fact, many big clothing retailers give end-of-line clothes to charities, or offer them at very low prices to staff. Some even destroy end-of-season stock to avoid undermining their original price position by being seen as a discounter.

You may think that this principle applies only to seasonal goods such as clothes, or perishable goods such as food, but it applies to anything the supplier wants to shift, whether that is to clear the shelves to make way for new stock, or just aid cashflow by getting rid of stock clogging up the warehouse.

The key point that needs to be understood is that the motivation of these big retail businesses is to clear the shelves, clear slow-moving items or to get rid of stock that will go out of date and be thrown away. They *are not discounting their prices as a strategy to improve sales volumes.*

Ouch!

These retailers have identified that their customers fall into a number of segments. Some are the *early movers* to whom they can sell the bulk of products at the highest prices. Then they will drop the price a little to sweep up the people that wanted the item but who weren't prepared to pay full price; ie the *price wary* customers, and they then get rid of what's left at little or no profit (but clear the shelves and avoid disposal costs) to the *bargain hunters*, or those whose decision is based on limited cash resources rather than any concern with the value for money.

What these retailers all know is that discounting prices does not simply generate increased sales, but it does moves the product value down to the next level of customer.

3 They made up the original price to make room for a discount

This issue is covered in depth in Chapter 8, so if you skipped that chapter go back and read it now.

There is nothing wrong with this approach. Manipulating prices to make consumers think that they are getting a great deal to capitalize on their natural desire to get a bargain is OK, providing you follow the legal rules. We would all like to think we had got something worth £1,000 for only £500, but the truth is that these are not *real* discounts.

The big downside of these practices is that it is conditioning consumers to believe that the profit margins businesses make are huge, based on the discounts they seem able to give. An ordinary local business that hasn't artificially inflated the price to start with must therefore overcome the customer's ignorance with better selling skills, or follow their example by inflating prices first. What you cannot do is give these high discounts unless they were built into your original price structure.

An accountant related this true story at a conference recently. A particularly difficult client was always arguing for a discount on the fees, to which the accountant had always steadfastly refused. Eventually he had enough and said:

> Dave, every year we have this same argument about discounts. So this year I have added on £800 to my normal prices, and as a result I can afford to give you a 10 per cent discount which is equal to £800. Is that OK?

The client was delighted that the accountant had finally caved in, despite the complete transparency that it had been added on first. The point was that it was never dissatisfaction with the value of the fees, just a desire to feel he had had a good deal.

4 Salespeople rush for a quick sale

Earlier chapters examined all of the elements that form part of the whole package of why a customer chooses to buy. Price is only one of the issues that need to be explained and explored with potential customers.

The trouble is that most of the people that businesses employ to sell are simply not appropriately trained to do that role. Once again, a whole other book could look at selling skills, but having looked at many businesses it is fair to say that on the whole salespeople have received far less training and personal development support than that role deserves and needs. The skills of your salespeople become ever more critical to your success if you are to overcome the Discounting culture.

Let's consider what a good salesperson should do; it will help us to see why there are so few. They should, for example:

✓ Prepare for the sales pitch with research into the potential customer, such as who are the decision-makers, what their business needs are, etc.

✓ Structure the call/sales pitch to ensure they get across the key points they want, and to uncover the needs/concerns of the customer.

✓ Take appropriate support material such as demonstration items, sales literature, brochures, etc.

✓ Be able to identify body language to know how to read a customer's reactions.

✓ Know when to go for the close. Too early or too late may miss the sale.

✓ Be ready. A great salesperson can adapt to any situation and is ready to sell at the drop of a hat. They can hear a buying signal like a pin dropping, and have business cards in the pocket of their pyjamas!

When these great salespeople sell, they will explore with a customer their needs, listen very carefully to all the customer's issues, and then explain how the features of the product or service they are selling will benefit the customer. They will cover issues such as when the item is needed, where it fits within the customer's business, when it must be delivered, acceptable quality tolerances, colours, sizes, quantities, and find out who else is a potential supplier. Price is of course one element that needs to be addressed, along with payment terms and any possible *volume* discount.

In simple terms a key cause of discounts in business is the poor skills of the frontline salespeople to sell properly, leaving price as the only bit left to work with. If you employ salespeople, or are one yourself, just think through the last time they went on a sales training course, read a book on body language, etc.

How to limit discounts

There is often resistance to the idea of controlling the ability of sales-people to give discounts. Many argue that it is like asking them to work with one hand tied behind their backs. It is crucial therefore to get these people to understand the issue with some blunt examples of the impact of giving them *free rein* to drop prices.

This case study is about a small plumbing business with a turn-over of £100k pa working for business customers and struggling with discounts.

CASE STUDY

Like many business owners Mr T was often in a position of having to give a discount to win the business (or at least he thought he had to). He was giving away almost £25k a year in discounts to be left with the £100k of turnover he actually billed. An external adviser convinced him to change his invoicing practices. In the past he would have agreed a sale of £125 and then a discount of £25 creating a net invoice of £100. This is the dialogue he tried:

I am sorry I can no longer give you a simple discount of 20 per cent, but I must invoice the £125 in full. However, as a valued customer I am still happy to do you a special deal, but I now have a 'cash back' policy if you pay promptly. I will give you £25 cash back so that you still in effect pay only £100. Sorry, but it's a new system my accountant has put in place.

Let me be clear that there is no intention to avoid VAT, etc, but just to change the customer's and the business's appreciation of the transaction, although we did insist that the rebate was actually done in cash.

So what changes?

- First, the customer previously felt that the item was only worth £100. Whatever the headline price, in his mind the discount was his right, and the real value was only ever £100. By separating the £25 and saying it is because he is a *valued customer* rather than it being seen as a price correction, the likelihood is that they will now appreciate the full value at £125 and the *bonus* of a £25 discount.

- If the customer ever needs to go back and look up the invoice to check what they paid, the odds are they will only find the £125 invoice and not the £25 credit note that accompanies the cash back element. They may therefore accept £125 *on a future purchase* without seeing it as a price hike, as they will see the £25 cash back as more of a one-off transaction.

- Most people like to get a surprise or something for nothing, and the impact of the cash back is to make the customer smile with the apparent *extra*. The key is that happier customers are more loyal, spend more, and recommend you.

- The plumber only gives the rebate and credit note at the point that the full invoice is settled. If there is a dispute of any kind, he can chase for the full debt. This helps to underline the payment-terms element of the sale. That is, why should someone that has taken 90 days to pay still get a discounted price?

- The selling business also now views the discount in a different way. When parting with real money, there is a clearer assessment of those customers who actually deserve it rather than those who demand it. When you actually give cash to some of your customers you will make much harsher judgements of who you are happy to give it to!

Let's be clear though: initially the plumber still only received the same £100 for the job. However, over time, this practice hardens his attitude towards who gets a discount and how much, and makes the customer far more appreciative of the amounts given. In many businesses this leads to significant reductions in the overall discounts given. Perhaps most importantly it enables the business to know how much discount they are giving away!

The logic of these points is simple common sense, although the practicalities of such an arrangement might bother you. It makes absolutely no difference to the turnover (£100 invoice, or £125 invoice with a £25 cash back), but it does affect both parties' appreciation of the deal.

Look back for a moment at the SE Limited case study and relate this issue to their business.

If they were to invoice at full value, and then offer a cash rebate, this would be an average of 21 per cent of the normal price. To do this they would need to have cash (real money, £10 notes, £1 coins, etc) totalling £6,650,000 over the course of a year; or £25,000 each working day. Clearly, this is impractical. They would need to employ a guard, there would need to be strict access controls and managing authorized access would become necessary.

Now the *Ouch!*

Yet when you look at most businesses that simply give discounts by knocking it off of the full price, you find almost always that *anyone* can give *any* level of discount, to *any* customer and for *any* reason and usually at the simple press of a button!

If a business didn't use cash back but allowed computer-generated discounts, then there is no lock on that door! The message to the sales force is *help yourself*!

Even in Mr T's business, the average discount of 20 per cent equates to £25,000, so this is his second biggest cost and if actually delivered in cash rebates it would still merit a big padlock on his office door!

Most businesses have far stricter controls on the £100 they keep in the petty cash tin than they do on tens of thousands, hundreds of thousands and even millions that they allow people to give away through uncontrolled discounts.

Ouch!

There is one final point on discounts that is covered in greater detail in Chapter 14 Getting Financial Clarity, but is important to mention here. Fine Worldwide Goods Limited undertook a project to improve its profitability. One of the first steps was to produce a spreadsheet of every single product, showing cost, list price and hence the expected profit margin.

The list had almost 5,000 lines of stock and looked like this:

FIGURE 10.4

Product List

Product	Cost	List price	Profit margin
a	£10.00	£15.00	£5.00
b	£12.00	£16.00	£4.00
c	£8.00	£14.00	£6.00
d	£14.00	£20.00	£6.00
e	£20.00	£35.00	£15.00
f	£34.00	£44.00	£10.00
g	£48.00	£75.00	£27.00

They then added a few more columns to show the average discount that had been given on those products to the various customers that bought them over the previous year. The list then looked like this:

FIGURE 10.5

Product List

Product	Cost	List price	Profit margin	Average discount	Discount amount	Revised margin
a	£10.00	£15.00	£5.00	20%	£3.00	£2.00
b	£12.00	£16.00	£4.00	35%	£5.60	-£1.60 ⬅
c	£8.00	£14.00	£6.00	25%	£3.50	£2.50
d	£14.00	£20.00	£6.00	30%	£6.00	£0.00
e	£20.00	£35.00	£15.00	30%	£10.50	£4.50
f	£34.00	£44.00	£10.00	0%	£0.00	£10.00
g	£48.00	£75.00	£27.00	40%	£30.00	-£3.00 ⬅

Notice the lines where the business was giving an average discount that was higher than the profit margin – meaning that these items were being sold at a gross loss.

How did this happen?

Many of their larger customers were given blanket discount rates of 30 per cent, based on the high total sales with that customer. Overall, these customers bought loads of items, most of which had 50 per cent or 60 per cent margins, and an average of 30 per cent discount seemed OK in view of the sheer volume they bought. However, some of the products they bought only had profit margins of 20 per cent or even 10 per cent. So although they may have been a profitable account overall, they were generating a profit on some products but losses on others.

This wasn't spotted because no one asked the right questions. You may think that this is a rare situation, but it happens in most businesses with a range of products or services.

> Thousands of businesses 'accidentally' give customers more discount than the profit they make on certain individual products or services.
>
> Ouch!

When discounting is right

It is important to address the issue that discounting is a valid tool in the salesperson's armoury.

In a perfect world a business would be able to charge a unique price to each individual customer based on all of the factors affecting them; ie their assessment of the value of the item, their ability to pay and perhaps the urgency to them. There may be 100 unique factors affecting each customer's perception of their side of the Value Scales.

If I can charge customer A a maximum of £100 for a product, but customer B is happy to pay £150 for the same item, then I want to charge them each their respective maximum.

What stops us from doing that is a variety of factors including the complexity of having different prices for different customers, and perhaps our own moral judgement of fairness. We also fear being *found out* by customer B and having no apparent justification for the differential.

In many businesses we get around these issues by charging the same headline price to all customers but giving varying discount levels to achieve the same thing. There is nothing wrong with this at all. This is as close as most businesses can get to the profit-maximizing approach of charging each customer a unique price.

The problem with this situation is all the points covered above. That is, there is no structure to the process, no control over individuals giving the discounts and no scoring of the amounts to understand what this costs the business each year, on each product line or for each customer.

So don't feel you have to abandon discounting as a tool to flex price properly for your different customers. It is a valid tool but it needs very careful management, and must be designed into your overall pricing strategy.

Summary

Businesses need to get much greater control over the issue. That means better systems and procedures, tighter rules and regulations, and discipline for the frontline people who actually give this money away. It is just too easy in most businesses to give discounts, and the pain associated with the press of a computer button or the stroke of a pen on the invoice simply doesn't equate to the actual amount of pain that *should* be felt from the drop in profit that follows the drop in price. If we can get the people on the frontline of a business to agree with the simple logic of the need to control discounts when they are real cash amounts, as in the case study of Mr T the plumber, then it is very hard for them to ignore this logic when it is only a number on a page or computer screen.

Minimizing discounts is a critical area of pricing strategy.

You must quantify the discounts that you give away, and have good rules or systems to control them.

Changing the way you use discounts as a tool to flex price for different customers is a valid pricing strategy, providing it is properly controlled and understood by all salespeople and any others involved in the process.

Action points

1 Quantify the amount of discounts that you are currently giving. Get the finance team to determine the full *list price* value of all that you sell and compare this with the turnover that you actually achieve. Set up a system that scores this in as much detail as possible; ie certainly in total, but perhaps by salesperson, by branch, by product line, by customer, etc, if this is possible with your accounting software.

2 Set time-bound targets on how much you want this reduced by (globally or by the same subcategories as in 1) and equate this to the impact on profits of successfully achieving it; ie a drop in discounts of 5 per cent might be an increase in profits of 50 per cent.

3 Develop discount rules for your business. For example:

- Discount levels for various team members, such as counter staff only authorized to give discounts up to 10 per cent without manager approval, managers can go to 20 per cent without director's approval, etc.

- Discounts not available where a customer account is outside of terms. That is, pay on time or pay more.

- Discounts must never be more than the profit margin being made.

- Discounts only with a minimum spend of say £100 or £1,000.

4 Once these rules have been approved by the CEO or finance team, have the pricing team design a roll-out plan so that the rules are communicated to the sales force, and in turn they communicate it to the customers.

5 Undertake discount-strategy training with all frontline people. Every one of those people must be able to explain the *discount vs volume* chart, and the other discounting issues covered. To demonstrate the magnitude of the discounting topic to your business, consider getting an average month's discount in real hard cash and putting it on the table during training.

6 Make someone responsible for this cost, a *Discount Controller*. Get them to identify who gives the most away, what are the most common reasons for giving that discount, are some customers getting too much? Make it their job to manage the cost down. In most businesses someone newly recruited at a cost of £30k a year could easily pay for themselves by tackling the issue properly.

7 Involve your HR people and link salespeople's performance-incentive pay to the gross margin achieved (after discounts) so they are driven to hold their nerve and limit the discounts they give.

11 Presenting the price properly

The early chapters covered the crucial aspect of making sure the salesperson emphasizes all of the features and benefits of any buying decision somewhere in the selling process. Quite simply, if a customer cannot appreciate all these issues, they will not add them to their side of the Value Scales in determining what they may be prepared to pay.

However, Chapter 8 did made the point that some customers are indeed motivated to buy by the *perception* of a great bargain. There is a familiarity with the comment by a person returning from a shopping spree saying, 'It was 50 per cent off so I bought two and saved twice as much!' Whether the purchase was necessary in the first place, or whether the discounted price was genuine or represented good value, is lost against the powerful feelings of getting a bargain.

This chapter explores the point that the presentation of the *price* itself is an equally important element in achieving the highest overall sale value and hence generating maximum profit for any business.

This chapter includes:

- The impact of the price ticket.

- The significance of clarity.

- Accuracy is key.

- The importance of the actual numbers.

- Presentation of price on bundled items.

- When to reveal your prices.

- Using words for impact.

The impact of the price ticket

In some retail environments the way in which a price is physically displayed can have an impact on how that price is perceived. A printed price ticket is read by customers as a real, *accurate* price that has been determined by someone who has worked it out properly, or even by a computer that has done some complex calculations to determine what the *right* price should be. If these price tickets look as though they have been properly printed – ie as you may find in a major electronics store on a new TV – then there is an underlying assumption that effort has been put into determining the price and producing the labels, so the price is probably *right* and unlikely to change. Rarely will customers question (in their heads or with a salesperson) a properly printed price ticket.

By contrast, a handwritten price ticket is taken as being someone's *judgement* of what the price should be, and hence may be seen by customers simply as a starting point. So in many small retailers a price ticket written out by the shop assistant or owner is sending the subconscious signal that it is negotiable.

Going further, a printed ticket that suggests a *calculated price*, but which has then been crossed through with a marker pen showing a new, lower, *handwritten* price, confers the message of a bargain deal. The customer accepts the validity of the original price but the hand-written correction suggests that the person who changed the price may be doing them a favour by overruling the *calculated* price on the printed ticket.

This engages the customer with the people in the business. Larger retailers use descriptions such as *Manager's Special Offer*, and you may have even seen some firms that put narrative such as *Head office won't like it, but the deal of the day is....* Now, don't think for a minute that head office are ignorant of the deal being done, but the presentation of the price in this way builds a rapport between the salesperson or branch, based on the perception that the customer is *getting one over* on the faceless managers in head office.

This is drifting into an area of *selling techniques* rather than the pure topic of pricing, but what is clear is that the way in which prices are expressed, and even the way in which they are displayed, can have a profound impact on customers' perceptions and hence the possibility that they will buy or not at various price levels.

The significance of clarity

Think back to the last time you went to buy something where the prices were not on display. That could have been perhaps a clothing store, jewellers or antiques shop, or an occasion where you were seeking advice from an accountant or lawyer.

How did you feel? What did you assume? What did you do?

Although your reaction may have been influenced by how keen you were to buy the product or service, on the whole people react in broadly similar ways:

Most people feel embarrassed to ask what the prices are! They feel that by doing so it might imply that they couldn't afford the item at certain price levels. We have all heard of those really top-end retail stores in London or Paris or, say, Rodeo Drive, where the suggestion is that *if you have to ask the price, then you can't afford it*!

The underlying assumption from most customers is that the products or services will be expensive. They believe that if the prices were *normal* – ie market rate, fair, reasonable, etc – then the business would be happy to display them or be open about what they are. By apparently hiding the price the assumption is that it must be unreasonably high.

What do most people do? They browse the shop for a short period, discreetly looking for prices on the bottom of items or hidden from view, and trying to make it look as though price doesn't matter to them, and that if they like it they would buy it regardless of the price. They then leave without asking a price, without knowing what any items cost and without buying anything.

Customers don't like uncertainty. However you opt to present your prices, you need to consider what image you are seeking to portray, what emotions you are trying to create within your customers (trust, perception of a bargain, a sense of urgency, etc), and then present your prices in the best way to achieve it.

Accuracy is key

One of the key factors in setting price is to use a number that demonstrates a degree of accuracy or certainty over the price itself.

Consider a homeowner who has asked a number of businesses to give a price for the installation of solar panels. Assume that there is no discernible difference between the products or services provided by all possible suppliers, and that they have not seen any significant differences in the sales material or the skills or perceived honesty of each salesperson. The decision to buy one of these has been made, and they can afford all options.

Focus now on the single issue remaining – price. The prices are so close that the amount is not an issue, and that there are no other discrepancies such as one business not charging VAT, for example. The decision as to which one to pick will be based solely on the *perception* of the business based on the way they have presented their price.

These five businesses have put forward their price offers as follows:

Business 1 – £5k all in.

Business 2 – £4,999, including VAT.

Business 3 – *About* £5,000.

Business 4 – *Between* £4,900 and £5,100, but we *won't know exactly* until we finish.

Business 5 – The *all-inclusive, fixed* price will be £4,173.68 + VAT so *exactly* £5,008.42.

How would most customers interpret these different choices? Just think for a moment before you read on as to which of the five options you would pick and why you would pick that one.

Business 4 is potentially the cheapest, but this is also possibly the most expensive. Let's explore them and consider what goes through the customer's mind when making the decision.

The use of the very round sum £5k *all in* description by Business 1 suggests that the price hasn't been properly worked out. It isn't even expressed as £5,000, but as an abbreviated £5k. This implies that it is an estimate based on a broad market price or *ballpark* figure. Most customers would assume one of two things: that it includes a high profit element, or there is a risk it may actually go up before the job is finished. This usually leads them to ask for further discounts, or to avoid the risk of an increase and shop elsewhere. It simply isn't believed as being a properly worked out price, and hence it isn't trusted as being fair or correct.

Business 2 has clearly been persuaded by the myth of the number 9 that was covered in Chapter 8, and thinks that the price of £4,999 will be seen by many customers as a *correct* price, being as it is just below the figure of £5,000. In fact, the larger the price, the less believable the issue of ending in a 9 becomes. It may work for items at £1.99 or £29.99, but it becomes counterproductive as the numbers get bigger and it seems completely contrived. At this level, customers will round up to the £5,000 anyway, and will probably feel that the business tried to trick them with a naive *fudged* price to make it look like a bargain. Consumers are not stupid and they know that the odds on a price being calculated fairly to cover the supplier's costs and make a decent profit are never going to end up £1 below a simple round sum amount.

Business 3 has destroyed completely the customer's confidence in the price it put forward, by the use of the word *about*. There are many businesses that use this or similar words such as *approximately* or use the word *estimate* rather than *quote*. This is a critical issue as consumers hate the uncertainty over price that these words bring. The natural assumption is that any actual price will always be higher than the estimate. So the supplier may be thinking that the price is *about* £5,000 because he doesn't know exactly how much cable he will need, so his final price could be £50 more or £50 less than the estimate. The customer, however, is thinking it will only ever be higher and that it may end up several hundred pounds more.

Business 4 has at least limited the range of the price uncertainty, and indicated that it could be lower, but there are two problems here. The first is that most customers will assume that the price will always be closest to the higher figure and that the supplier is trying to mislead them by giving the range but intending to bill the top price anyway. This may push some customers to buy elsewhere, even though the price *could* be the lowest option. The second problem is with the customers who set their expectation at the lower end of the scale and become unhappy customers once a higher price is finally received, despite the openness of the supplier up front. In most businesses, leaving any uncertainty on price will either push the customer away, or lead to retrospective arguments. It is a recipe for problems.

So whether it is a single number that is then weakened by the word *about* or *estimate*, or a range that has inherent uncertainty built in, customers prefer to avoid uncertainty or they assume the worst anyway and make their judgement based on the top price indicated.

Business 5 has set a price that implies a number of things. First, that it is absolutely fixed in stone and that the customer can have confidence that this will indeed be the amount that they pay. Second, the accuracy of the amount, even down to the final 42 pence, suggests that this is a carefully worked out price that reflects all of the costs of the job. Most of us understand that when we buy something, the business must make a profit, but we want to feel that the profit level is fair. Using very specific numbers gives a clear suggestion that all the components of the deal have been properly considered, including a fair profit level.

Although it may vary from product to product, customers also want to feel that they are getting the same sort of deal other customers get. When we see round sum numbers or price ranges, there is sometimes a concern that the price may have been uniquely assessed just for us and perhaps increased based on a perception of our ability to pay; ie they may worry that the solar panel price is higher for a house with a brand new Porsche on the drive than it would be for an identical installation on a house with a single 10-year-old car on the drive. When we hear very specific numbers we simply assume that the price is the properly calculated price for that job, irrespective of our circumstances, and has not been *plucked out of thin air*!

Let's look at this from a slightly different perspective. In Chapter 10 we discussed the problem of discounts. Let's now look at why *accuracy* in discounting is essential.

Premier Wholesale Limited is a £1m turnover business selling tools and equipment to trade customers. Dave, the Sales Manager, was on the phone to a relatively new customer who was clearly asking the question about a discount.

From outside his office, only Dave's side of the conversation was audible and went like this:

Dave: Yes we have that in stock, I can ship it today.

Pause

Dave: *Normally* that model sells for £1,000 + VAT.

Pause

Dave: Yes, OK we can do something on the price, how about 30 per cent off?

Pause

Dave: No. 30 per cent is what everybody gets.

Pause

Dave: Great I will get it sorted immediately.

What had actually happened was that the customer had asked, 'Can you do a deal?' Dave had gone straight to a 30 per cent discount rather than starting at a lower amount, because 'almost everyone gets 30 per cent so it is easy to work out the adjusted prices'.

As soon as he said *normally*, he was sending a very loud signal that there was room for negotiation. Simply stating what the price *is* reduces that risk enormously. Once a negotiation is underway, there is a key need for good negotiating skills to keep the downward movement in price as low as possible.

This is typical of many salespeople. Whether they start at 30 per cent or less, almost all discounts will be a simple number of 10 per cent, or perhaps 20 per cent, and almost always a multiple of 5. This is not because it's the right answer, it's because it is easy for the salesperson to calculate!

The major problem with these round sum discounts is that no one believes them. If a customer asks for a good deal, and the salesperson says 'I can do 20 per cent' the chances are the customer still thinks there may be some further flexibility in the price. In fact, in the real example, even starting at 30 per cent, the customer still pushed further. This would be true if he had said 5 per cent, 10 per cent or 15 per cent, in fact any 'round sum' multiple. Just like the examples above of the *round sum* approach to the headline price, round sum discount figures are assumed to be made-up numbers.

Let's see how the conversation could have gone:

Dave: Yes we have that in stock, I can ship it today.

Pause

Dave: *Normally* that sells for £1,000 + VAT.

Pause

Dave: (after loud random tapping on calculator) I could do a special price just for you based on the specific machine you are buying, and on the understanding that you will pay on time, with a discount from list price of 21.27 per cent. On this machine, that means you will pay £787.30.

Now how would you feel if you were the customer? Obviously, you would prefer 30 per cent, but if you didn't know it was available and the proposal of 21.27 per cent was made, you are much more likely to believe that this is the *right* price based on the sheer accuracy of the numbers, and the apparent *calculation* of them. What is more, the business has clearly linked the discount to a specific machine, not necessarily for all products, and only if paid on time. This enables the company to quote different discounts for future products and even cancel the discount if the customer fails to pay on time.

This was tried on the next sale, and although not a truly scientific comparison, the second customer did accept the 21.27 per cent discount offered without challenge. The financial impact of this 8.73 per cent reduction (30 per cent down to 21.27 per cent) in the discount was massive. In this example reducing the price by £212.70 rather than £300.00, added an extra £87.30 of sales value, and meant that the gross profit they made on that machine went from £250.00 up to £337.50, a 35 per cent increase. Once again it was simply a matter of taking time to sell properly, and present the price in a more sophisticated way.

Another business actually prohibited the idea of round sum discounting. 5 per cent, 10 per cent, 15 per cent, 20 per cent, 25 per cent, etc, were simply no longer allowed. If a customer wanted 10 per cent, the salesperson now had to get them to agree to 9 per cent or 11 per cent. The salespeople were bemused and challenged the fact that if a customer expected 10 per cent, and would just not accept a 9 per cent discount, that they would actually prefer to give away 11 per cent. This was confirmed to be the case.

The point, of course, was to make the salespeople *think*. Over a period of time, forcing them to discuss the available discounts with customers, and as a result sell on features and benefits rather than a simple *I'll knock off another 5 per cent or 10 per cent*, would bring the discounts down and as a result, the real prices up.

In this company they found that the salespeople got into the habit of talking more directly about the price, and where they once typically gave 20 per cent, they didn't just drop to 19 per cent, but gradually they got down to 18 per cent, then 17 per cent, and then to 16.73 per cent, etc. Eventually the average discount reduced by almost a quarter. This was simply because it was made difficult for salespeople to revert to giving standard discounts. Also, they were trained to talk more to the customer, discuss more openly the issue of price and, of course, pick a number that had a more credible feel than the old *round sum* numbers previously used. When they used to say 20 per cent, many customers often asked for 25 per cent. When they said a very specific 17.4 per cent, no one pushed for more.

The importance of the actual numbers

You will recall the myth surrounding the significance of the number 9, which was that the power of this number was in its being psychologically below a key price threshold and hence giving a perception of being great value for money.

A major experiment in the USA tested the impact of certain prices on customer demand. They worked with a major mail order catalogue company to test the demand of particular products at differing prices. For example, a ladies fleece jacket was offered for sale with a great picture and positive narrative in around 60,000 catalogues across its customer base. In one third of the catalogues the price was shown as $44, in another third it was priced at $49 and in the last third it was priced at $54.

The distribution of the catalogues was random, such that three neighbours might each have one with a different price. The jacket cost the company $20 to buy in, so they made either $24, $29 or $34 of profit per item.

Let's look at the results:

Price of jacket	Volume sold	Profit generated
$44	1,000	$24,000
$49	1,500	$43,500
$54	1,000	$34,000

There are two interesting conclusions here. First, that the $44 and $54 prices sold the same volumes, suggesting that high or low price did not have any impact on the sales volumes. It was perhaps the great picture, good narrative or position in the catalogue that was having the impact on the sales of that jacket compared to others, rather than being a price-based decision. This confirms a lot of what this whole book preaches; ie it isn't all about being cheaper.

The second interesting point that the university conducting the study concluded, was that people prefer a price with a 9 at the end of it. As explained already, 9 is a familiar and trusted number and it might be easy to conclude that it is the number itself that is the key. But all the university study really showed was that 9 was a more popular or more significant number than the number 4. The question is whether it is more significant than, say, the number 3 or the number 8.

Ask people to score something on a scale of 1 to 10 (where 10 is excellent) and the vast majority will score 7. That is because it is the number least likely to provoke a follow up question such as 'only a 6, what was wrong?' or 'an 8, what in particular did you like?'

> We attended a seminar that looked at the power of numbers in selling to customers, and were really gripped by the point that 7 is a non-confrontational and hence powerful number.
>
> As a result, we simply made sure that every single quote we sent out ended in a number 7. This could be a quote we might have sent out for exactly £10,000 being changed to show £10,007 instead.
>
> We were amazed at the improvement in our conversion rate for the quotes we won. Although many customers asked to round the price down by the *odd* 7 pounds, very few argued about the overall price.
>
> Sarah Hill Builders

The major point is this. The actual numbers that you use to express the price of the goods or services that you sell have a direct impact on whether the buyer believes the validity of the price and ultimately whether they are prepared to pay it. There is a very real danger that any round sum presentation, whether of headline price or discount percentages or £ price reductions, undermines the customer's perception that the prices are real, fair, properly calculated or non-negotiable.

An item priced at £10.07 will be more attractive to customers than one priced at £10.00. Whether it is more attractive that £10.09 or £9.99 is not as clear-cut. This contrasts completely with many businesses that set their prices by trying to simplify the presentation to the customer using round sum prices or round sum percentage discounts.

Presentation of price on bundled items

Chapter 6 looked at the idea of bundling products in order to encourage customers to buy additional items within a bundle that they may not have bought if they were able to make a decision on an item-by-item basis. One of the key issues for businesses is the presentation of this bundled price.

Let's make a very basic comparison between a menu of choices, and a bundled deal. On the whole a menu of prices gives the advantage to the customer as it allows them to individually assess the elements they want and the value for money to them of each separate component. In most cases this will mean that some customers will opt out of at least some of the options that the supplier wanted to sell. From the customer's perspective, unbundled or menu pricing creates transparency and allows them to select exactly the options they want.

Conversely, bundling helps the seller. First, there is the simplicity of a single-priced bundle, so that if you can sell the same bundle to everyone, it makes life easier. The easier it is to package, sell and deliver the bundled items, the lower the marketing and selling costs. Bundling also means that customers assess the total value and end up buying elements they may have opted not to buy on a menu-priced basis.

When a seller unbundles options it opens up the whole transaction to line-by-line scrutiny. If, for example, a plumber had agreed a price with a client for fitting out a bathroom at £5,750, the customer will make a judgement about the overall value of the work versus the price being asked. Now say the plumber presents a bill listing the individual hours spent on each aspect of the work by each tradesperson, each individual item from bath to taps and tile adhesive, and also includes an amount for removing waste, ordering parts, etc. Even though the total price is exactly what was quoted, the reality is that many customers will review the detailed list of items and will almost certainly baulk at some elements, such as the fact that two workers took the scrap to the tip charging two lots of time. Even if they were happy with the overall price before, they may become dissatisfied now that they can see some individual items they think are overpriced.

By contrast, there is a desire for some businesses to list out every component of the bundle in order to demonstrate clearly the overall value of the package. Like the examples given in Chapter 6, Microsoft want to make it very clear what each individual piece of software costs so that they can tempt customers into buying the *Home Office* package for a much better overall price.

So what should you do? Hide the individual prices into a single bundled price without any explanation of the component elements? Show the bundled price and each of the components so customers can assess the savings the bundle represents, or offer the customer a menu to pick and choose what they want?

The simple answer is that *it depends*. Look at the Action Points and see what you could do to test this for your business.

What you need to do is look at the things you sell and identify how these could be bundled together. Initially you should look at what you do to see whether there may be some obvious bundling opportunities. However, in many businesses it is the act of seeking to develop compelling packages that leads them to try and find new features and benefits to add into a bundle in order to add the value to the customer. So although it may be obvious that where you sell products that link together – such as a PC, printer, anti-virus software, etc – great bundles can be developed, many other businesses can develop some excellent bundles with special service elements. In an earlier chapter we looked at the computer software company that bundled in training, post-sale support, and a later review of any changed requirements.

When to reveal your prices

If your business is essentially retail, where customers are free to browse (in-store or online) then you must show the price clearly and if you want to offer discounts, be clear on the terms and conditions that apply.

As discussed above, keeping the price under wraps in these sorts of situation creates uncertainty and often steers the customer to look elsewhere.

If you are in a service business where price may vary uniquely for each customer (a legal firm or kitchen fitter, for example), or in a business-to-business operation where negotiation is expected, then you need to be a little careful about talking price too soon.

It is essential to consider all of the elements that go onto the customer's side of the Value Scales, and all the features and benefits of doing business with you, before you look at the price on your side of the scales. The end objective remains the same; ie to get the scales to balance so that customer and supplier agree on the price and *value*, or to tip them slightly in favour of the customer so that they have a perception of getting a *good deal*. However, it is harder to move the scales from tipped entirely in your favour (price is on but nothing else has been said) towards the customer by gradually adding all of the value points for them.

Much better to tip the scales completely in the favour of the customer by loading all the value points on first and then seeing if your price tips it the other way.

> Make sure the customer is clear on the value you offer before you tell them the price.

There is a word of warning though. If you take this to the extreme, as some businesses do, you create a lack of trust as the customer can feel you are trying to trick them by avoiding a direct dialogue about the price.

There is a true story about one situation where a couple had to *demand* a price from a kitchen company who just kept reworking designs and talking about all the clever features they could include, steadfastly avoiding the question of price until the couple simply refused to discuss anything further. Through that process they lost all confidence in the salesperson and, regardless of the value of the kitchen they offered, would never have bought from them.

So when you get the clear signal that the customer wants to talk price, get it on the table straight away. In many cases this is a buying signal that is ignored at great cost.

Using words for impact

Once you have addressed all of the points above, there is a further subtlety to the issue of price presentation. There are many ways to say the word *price*, and each will have a slightly different impact in the mind of the customer.

Price, for example, is a clear statement of the amount that the customer is expected to pay. It does not make any comment on the value of that item, or the potential benefit to the customer of paying it.

If you use words such as *current* price, or *this week's* price, or *today's* special, you make it clear that the price may go up, and that creates a sense of urgency in the mind of the customer. The quicker you get a customer to buy, the better.

Using terms such as *your investment* when you talk about an accountancy service, for example, will get the customer to consider the amount in context with ongoing or long-term benefits of buying the advice.

The word *fee* is mostly used in professional firms and adds a layer of credibility based on the assumption that professionals can be trusted. If a lawyer talked about a legal case and referred to the *price* of the work, the customer's perception of quality would be reduced.

The dictionary is full of words that can be added in to the mix and which present a particular message to customers. You may have seen many prices promoted with additions such as *crazy*, *outrageous*, *incredible* and many other adjectives that underline a purported value for money.

These terms will apply differently to each business depending on its products and services, its typical customers and the image it is seeking to promote about the business as a whole.

Summary

The way that you express the price can have a dramatic impact on the customer's willingness to pay it.

Making a price clear and understandable, as well as accurate and believable, will remove a great deal of the downward pressure on prices caused by customers seeking to avoid uncertainty.

Action points

1 Change all of your prices and discounts anywhere that round sum figures are undermining the credibility of your overall message.

2 Look at all the ways your prices are described and develop and implement a range of descriptions that express your prices more positively; ie *investment* rather than *cost*.

3 Review the way all of your prices are displayed. Does it suggest to the customer that there is room for negotiation? Is it clear and unambiguous to them? Implement changes to add clarity and certainty to the presented price.

4 Undertake a review of how all of your major competitors describe their prices and adopt their good practices into your business. Ensure your sales team are trained to exploit any uncertainty they may create in the way they express prices.

12 Directional pricing

We have previously looked at how customers make choices to buy your product or service instead of those of your competitors, and at how to get them to buy more, or to simply pay more for the things that they do buy. As we have seen, there are many elements to the decision to buy, of which price is only one. You need to understand that price can be a positive tool in winning a sale rather than just a route of dropping the price to make the Value Scales balance.

Chapter 6 looked at the idea of bundling items together into packaged prices in the belief that offering a wider range of options will allow our premium customers to buy a premium solution, while our value customers buy our cheaper options. This chapter is specifically focussed on how we can use price as a lever to deliberately move customers from one product or service to another. There are a number of benefits to this, which will be presented.

Essentially, the idea of directional pricing is to encourage customers to buy the products that *you* want them to buy, by using price as a way of discouraging them from buying other products or encouraging them to buy the ones that you want.

This chapter includes:

- The advantages of moving customers to alternative options.
- The pizza example.
- The critical issues to know.
- Setting extreme prices to make other offers seem comparatively attractive.

The advantages of moving customers to alternative options

Before we look at the *how?* part of this chapter we need to consider the *why?* part. What are the benefits of moving a customer to buy one option or another by adjusting price to encourage them to do so?

- Reducing stock levels – To get customers to buy more of one particular product in an effort to turn the value tied up in this excess stock into cash, liberate shelf space or dispose of stock you fear may perish in the short term. Adjusting the price of this, or of alternative products, may have an impact on how much of the target product we shift.

- Up-selling – Getting customers to buy a higher quality and hence higher priced item because the total value of the sale increases; ie in the earlier lawnmower example, the gross profit percentage was the same on all options, but the more expensive options clearly generated a higher £ value of profit.

- Steering customers to more profitable items – Getting customers to buy a product or service that is more profitable than the alternatives. This may not necessarily be a higher priced item, but is one on which the profit may be greater.

- Tying in with future revenues – Persuading the customer to buy a product where there may be further ongoing revenues from which additional future profits can be derived. Again, using the lawnmower example, there was a greater potential for ongoing revenues from the petrol mower options with servicing compared to the probable *once only* sale of an electric lawnmower.

Once again, most of this is actually a sales skill that needs to be honed and used by the frontline people, but price is a factor in the decision-making that can be very influential in directing the customer to one purchase over another.

The pizza example

A project to drive up the profits of a struggling tourist attraction, DFAP, considered the profitability of the main food outlet on the site. Initial research found a number of important issues. Problems included issues such as that the seating area was right next to the indoor play area, and tables were often clogged up by people just drinking tea or coffee while their children played in the play area, or worse still, they just used a table and made no purchases from the restaurant at all.

Furthermore, when customers looked into the restaurant seating area, they were often put off from ordering food due to the absence of somewhere to sit, or just the perception that it was exceptionally busy and would take a long time to be served. Although this is not at face value a price issue, customers paying restaurant prices for their meal expected to be able to sit at a table to eat it. Without this, the Value Scales tipped the wrong way and often drove customers to use the outdoor fast food options of sandwiches and snacks where sales values and margins were lower.

Freeing up the restaurant space to enable customers to see the value of an indoor sit-down meal option was crucial.

We were then able to look at the individual food offers and consider points, such as the raw material cost of the product and hence the gross profit margin. We also observed the time it took to produce and therefore the wage costs and the impact on the speed through the service area and tills.

The conclusions were fairly obvious:

- French fries (chips!) were a high-margin product. In high demand, and easy to produce quickly by cooking them constantly without a high risk of wastage from over-production.

- Pizzas were reasonably high margin, but it took almost the same ingredient cost, cooking time and labour cost to produce a Small, Medium or Large one. Therefore the larger pizzas were significantly more profitable that the smaller ones.

- Once we had a customer in the restaurant, the table was taken for, say, 30 minutes; the ordering process, cash-handling activities and the table clearing were almost the same whether a family bought just chips and a can of drink for each of them, or whether they bought pizzas, burgers, chips, hot drinks and ice creams as part of a full meal for the family.

Clearly, what we wanted to do was to encourage guests to buy more of the profitable items and spend more overall.

The chapter on bundling looked at the idea of packaging items together to encourage customers to spend more, and in this context we did develop a number of *meal deal* options that offered say a Small pizza, fries and a cold drink at a competitive price compared to the individual components. That is, individually the pizza could be £3.99, fries £1.50 and a drink £1, but the total of £6.49 would be reduced to £5.99 on the meal deal option. This did indeed lead to increasing the average value of each sale. If you want to see a business that is brilliant at this then just visit your nearest McDonald's!

However, in the context of this chapter I just want to explore how we used directional pricing to affect the sales of pizzas.

Although they sold Small, Medium and Large sizes of pizza, they found that the large pizzas were usually bought by families to share, so they focussed their attention on the Small- and Medium-sized options to see if they could improve profit by using directional pricing techniques.

When they calculated the profit on these two pizza choices they found the following data:

TABLE 12.1*

	Cost to produce	Selling price	Profit	Percentage sold
Small pizza	£2.90	£4.00	£1.10	50 per cent
Medium pizza	£3.20	£5.00	£1.80	50 per cent

*Numbers are simplified to make the maths easier and to make the point crystal clear. Please don't get hung up on whether the items should have been priced at £3.99 or £4.99!

What we can see from this data is that the costs of producing a Medium pizza are only marginally above the Small one, just an extra £0.30. The labour costs to make them and the cooking time are almost identical, and there is only a small extra cost for the additional ingredients. Given the extra £1 on the price, the profit was clearly better on the Medium pizza.

Now, you would obviously want to sell more Medium pizzas than Small ones, as each one makes around £0.70 more profit, partly because its price was higher but also because the margin was 36 per cent compared to only 27.5 per cent on the smaller one.

When they looked at the numbers, they found that they sold almost exactly the same number of each size. What this told us was that overall, the extra price of £1 was seen as a fair uplift to match the extra value of the bigger size; ie the Value Scales balanced properly for each pizza.

But it is not the business's objective to ensure that every item sold is priced *fairly* with others; the objective is to deliver value and make a profit. The question is therefore: *What can we do to encourage customers to move from the small pizza to the medium pizza where we make a higher profit?*

The box below explains four options and the *risks* with each. These need to be considered with the inherent uncertainty that we could not work out customer reaction in advance, and would therefore need to take a leap of faith and test an idea in a real-life situation.

---

1 *Free extra toppings on the Medium pizza* – Adding extra mushrooms or bacon bits at a cost of 10p has a low impact on the profit margin (£1.80 reduces to £1.70, or 36 per cent reduces to 34 per cent) but it differentiates the value between each option.

The risk with this option is that it would have added an extra £0.10 to the cost of all the Medium pizzas, and if no one upgraded from the Small to the Medium we would have just reduced our overall profits unnecessarily. It is a low risk in the sense that we could trial it for a week and see what happened and then simply remove the *special offer* sign if it didn't work.

2 *Increase the cost of the Small pizza* – We knew already that customers thought that the extra £1 on the price was matched by the extra value of the Medium size, hence the 50:50 split in sales volumes. Therefore, if we set the price of the small at, say, £4.50, many customers may upgrade to the Medium-sized one as a result of the perception of much greater value compared to the new price of the Small one.

   This is a little more risky as some customers may not upgrade to the Medium or even stick with the Small at the new higher price, but might simply opt out altogether and not buy either pizza. The reality of course is that they would probably buy something else instead, such as a burger. So again, a modest risk of losing customers overall.

3 *Decrease the price of the Medium pizza* – The value-for-money issue is the same as the point above; ie if we know that customers currently see the price and value differential as fair, so that dropping the Medium price to, say, £4.80 should nudge a few customers to move from the Small up to the Medium, and we would still be making a higher profit on the larger pizza.

   This is a lower risk in the sense of upsetting customers, but like option 1, if we failed to move enough customers from the Small to the Medium by making it seem much better value, then we have just given profit away from all those customers who already bought the higher priced item.

4 *Removing the Small option altogether* – People who specifically wanted a pizza would have no choice but to buy the Medium (or the large family-sized option) because the less profitable Small option is no longer on offer.

   This is a similarly risky option as number 2, in that some customers may not buy the Medium in the absence of the Small option, but in a captive location such as the tourist attraction they would probably buy something else instead. The added advantage for the business is the simplicity of now offering fewer choices and therefore gaining a little simplicity on the menu, making preparation a little quicker and easier.

None of the options are without some risk, either in losing customers or in giving profit away that is not matched by customers opting to buy the more profitable pizza.

We increased the Small pizza by 50 pence. The figures then looked like this:

TABLE 12.2*

	Cost to produce	Selling price	Profit	Percentage sold
Small pizza	£2.90	£4.50	£1.60	40 per cent
Medium pizza	£3.20	£5.00	£1.80	60 per cent

*Again, numbers are simplified to make the maths easier and to make the point crystal clear.

As you can see from the above, the costs of production are unchanged, the profit on each item is now very similar and the profit margin within a 1 per cent range. Essentially the business didn't now care which one customers bought as they were happy with the profit on either.

As you can also see from the end column, the impact was to move approximately 10 per cent of the customers from the Small to the Medium option. What did that mean in overall profit terms?

Old Prices
50 small pizzas at £1.10 profit on each   £55
50 medium pizzas at £1.80 profit on each   £90
Total profit for 100 pizzas   £145

New Prices
40 small pizzas at £1.60 profit on each   £64
60 medium pizzas at £1.80 profit on each   £108
Total profit for 100 pizzas   £172

As you can see, we were able to increase the gross profit for each batch of 100 pizzas from £145 to £172. This was an increase of almost 18.6 per cent.

That is the essence of *directional pricing*.

The critical issues to know

The most critical issue with the principle of directional pricing is to make sure you know the current facts before you consider tinkering with the prices. You absolutely need to know the exact profit you make on every item you sell. That is not just as simple as the gross profit on each one (although that is a very good starting place) but should cover things such as the impact of returns by customers, or complementary sales. In other words, it is no good pushing customers to buy product A that seems to be more profitable if that item is frequently returned for refunds, or if product B generates significant future revenues. The lawnmower business may have one brand of mower that generates more profit but which is forever breaking down within the warranty period, or may prefer to sell a lower profit petrol mower than a higher profit electric one that has no ongoing service and maintenance revenues.

When you know the true profit on each item, you also need to know the numbers you sell of each. In many businesses this could be a simple button-pressing exercise to interrogate the computer, but in the pizza example the till records simply said *pizza* until we made them show the specifics of the size. We could identify the volumes based on the prices but it is a lot easier if the computer or smart till can spit out the numbers.

When you know these facts, you need to establish what economists call the *elasticity of demand* for the products. That is, its sensitivity to price. In other words, what will be the impact on sales volumes as prices rise or fall? The problem of course is that there is no book with this data. It will vary from business to business and customer to customer, and even day to day. What you need to do is to test it by good old-fashioned trial and error.

The starting point is to identify products or services where customers could choose option A or option B based on their perception of value. That could be as simple as Small- or Medium-sized pizza, or it could be any pizza versus any burger. In Chapter 6 we looked at the example of a professional services firm that offered Gold-, Silver- or Bronze-level options containing different service levels, such as variations on the frequency of contact.

When you know the true costs and profit of alternative options, and you are clear on where customers can choose option A or B, then you can start to explore the impact of using price to move customers to the one you want them to buy.

My suggestion would be to test this gently by talking with a few trusted customers to ask their views on value for money; ie would they buy option A or B at £X prices, and would that decision change if the prices changed to £Y.

You could also test prices on individual customers or groups that are already unprofitable and where you may therefore accept an outcome of losing the customer altogether. Or you could test it on a branch-by-branch basis where you have multiple outlets and compare the results from each.

There is, however, a very important point that must be understood. In earlier chapters we looked at the fact that most businesses are already charging below the level of the customer's real view of value. This lack of confidence to charge the right price is a fundamental problem for many businesses. Therefore, a basic strategy for many businesses is just to nudge the prices up slightly and see what happens. In my experience of a great many businesses, nothing happens. Customers accept the higher price and the business simply makes more money. The changes are so small and the existing value so high that customers just don't react. The object of directional pricing is that we want them to react. We want them to choose a more profitable option as our pricing has either made that option appear much better value for money or the alternative option much worse value, encouraging them to switch. Therefore, small changes in price are unlikely to give us any really valuable data to assess customers' reactions to price.

If we had changed the price of the pizzas to, say, £4.03 and £4.97 (once again ignoring the significance of numbers or price thresholds covered in earlier chapters) the reality is that we may have seen no measurable change in the volumes and concluded that there was no point in pressing on with the plan.

> What many projects that look at pricing tell us is that very few businesses even think about the idea of encouraging customers to buy their most profitable products, and are just pleased that they have bought anything at all!
>
> Ouch!

If you combine the thinking on the issues covered in Chapter 6 with some additional effort to consider the points covered in this chapter, many businesses will be able to develop bundled options that are priced in such a way as to ensure customers are encouraged to pick the ones that generate the most profit. All it really requires is clarity on the financials and a desire to try.

Setting extreme prices to make other offers seem comparatively attractive

The final point I want to make is the situation where we use a very high top-end price to encourage customers to buy a lower-priced option by creating an impression of exceptional value for money.

CASE STUDY

A small plumbing business specializes in installing bespoke bathrooms for individual customers. Typically, the price for a standard fit-out may be between £5k to £10k depending on what bathroom the customer wants and their choice of quality of fittings, etc. Ordinarily the business owner would simply offer options in the range of £5k to £10k and then debate with the customer what they want and what they can afford. This may be presented as say Gold, Silver or Bronze levels as described previously. The customer will make their selection based on their own personal perception of the Value Scales at each price point.

What happens if we now add a *Platinum option* at £25k?

It does several things. First, it suggests that that the plumber is certainly capable of delivering a Wow! bathroom that is out of this world. This gives the customer much greater confidence that he is more than capable of delivering any of the lower-priced options to very high standards; ie it adds credibility to the *quality* message that the plumber wants to convey.

Second, by just having a £25k option, the plumber makes the £10k option seem much better value for money compared to when that was the top-of-the-range price. A customer who was thinking *£10,000 seems a lot*, will no longer see that amount as so expensive. Although it may not change their ability to afford any option, they will certainly see the £10k choice as better value for money than when it was the top price.

Finally, he might occasionally be amazed by a customer who says, 'Great – go ahead with the £25k option!'

Many businesses would benefit by adding a very high top-end option to the choices the customer has because, regardless of whether any of them buy it, the perception of value for all other choices increases.

A business selling large, garden play equipment had a range of products that stretched from around £1,000 to almost £10,000 in price. They found it really hard to get many customers to select the most expensive option, until they added the absolute child's dream of a garden castle costing almost £16,000. Over the following year they only sold one of these top-of-the-range options, but the sales of the previously most expensive choice more than doubled.

Summary

With any business, the number one priority is to try and achieve a sale. Once the seller is in the area where that is possible – ie the Value Scales are moving around the balanced position, they should then be considering what *they want to sell*. That may be driven by a motivation to shift particular lines of slow-moving stock, or to sell a more profitable option to the customer.

This is where directional pricing comes into play: flexing the prices of the various options our customers could choose, as a lever to nudge them towards the products we want to sell.

If the business's motivation is to try and shift slow-moving stock, this is almost always done by simply dropping the price of those items, when this may be just as easily achieved by increasing the price of the alternatives.

If the motivation is to use directional pricing to increase the overall profit, then the problem is that there are rarely sufficient facts about profit margins to use this tool properly. Before a business can even consider playing around with prices to direct customers from one product to another, they absolutely need to know exactly what profits they make on each one.

If you combine these issues with the guidance in Chapter 6 on how to bundle items and offer variations of these to customers, then directional pricing techniques can be a powerful tool in any pricing strategy.

Action points

1 Make sure you know the profit margin of every product or service that you sell.

2 When you have the information from 1, you should then identify who should have access to this information so that it is properly used. The pricing team will need to set target prices, maximum discounts figures, etc and to determine prices of comparable items as part of the directional pricing approach. However, be careful that the facts on profits are not simply used by frontline people to *sell down* to the lowest level possible to achieve a sale.

3 Identify any items for which there is a current need to promote sales. That may be based on high stock levels or potential obsolescence. Review prices to encourage sales of these items (ie lower price if you buy 10 items, rather than a lower price overall).

4 Diarize a repeat of action three- or six-monthly or at quarterly intervals so that you have a rolling programme of stock clearances.

5 Identify all products where customers can choose to purchase two or more similar items (eg petrol or electric lawnmowers or Gold, Silver and Bronze options) and where they therefore make a choice as to which one they buy. For these items:

   a Ensure you know the profit you make on each option (see 1).

   b Identify any additional issues such as the potential for ongoing revenues or associated purchases.

   c Identify your preferences as to which product you wish to prioritize for sale.

   d Get the pricing team to set price variances to test how you can move customers to your preferred option.

   e Once the pricing team are happy with the results at d, get them to train frontline staff appropriately and update all relevant sales materials.

6 Make sure your current systems are capable of identifying sales by line items on your products or services lists; ie Small pizzas vs Medium pizzas rather than just pizzas.

7 Look at all of the products and services you sell and identify a Platinum option that can be added to your price lists in order to improve the perception of value for all other choices.

Dealing with the human factor

13

Inevitably, any action in a business will have human involvement. This includes many elements of behaviour, such as avoidance of fear and the pursuit of pleasure, and of course a wide variation of personal characteristics such as honesty, confidence, diligence, etc.

This chapter could therefore be the one that you find the hardest to read. Whereas it is easy for us to see and understand these traits in others, we rarely acknowledge that we also share some of the more negative characteristics ourselves.

Although everyone is unique, there are some very real and common characteristics that apply to most of the people, most of the time. So try to think of these issues as they may apply to your colleagues and your customers, rather than get hung up on the issue of whether they apply to you personally. Once you accept that these characteristics are valid and need to be managed in others, it may be much easier to adopt some of the messages that may apply to you.

This chapter includes:

- Most people running a business are untrained for that role.
- Conscious competency.
- Don't be afraid to get external input.
- The key people in the profit equation.
- Handling your team's need to please customers.
- Helping your team focus on profit.
- Dealing with the human factor in your customers.
- Fear!

Most people running a business are untrained for that role

Probably the most significant human factor in any business improvement project is that the vast majority of business people have had no formal training in *how* to run a business. There are a few people who have earned themselves an MBA, and then applied this theoretical knowledge to a real business, or who have worked in huge organizations and had the opportunity to take part in on-the-job development training specific to that business. The reality is, however, that perhaps more than 95 per cent of business owners and managers have *never* been formally trained on how to run a business. The majority of business owners and managers are simply making it up as they go along.

Now that isn't the point. I am not suggesting that there should be a test to pass before you are allowed to run a business, although perhaps there may be a valuable lesson to learn from the professions such as lawyers and accountants who have a minimum standard of entry, examinations to test competency, and ongoing requirements to keep the qualification. But there is no problem with business owners and managers learning their skills in real time and in real-world situations.

The problem is more that each one of these people thinks that they are the only one learning their skills this way. They go to work every day with the nagging doubt that someone somewhere will suddenly catch them out and say, *hey, you're not qualified to do that job*!

If I had a pound for every time I have had someone say, 'This may be a stupid question, but...'. Of course, the stupid bit is to not ask a question when you don't understand something, based on a fear of looking silly. (That may be an *Ouch!* moment for you.)

What this often creates, though, is a feeling of insecurity. Business owners, directors and managers feel uncomfortable putting their hands up and saying *run that by me again, I really didn't get that*, or *sorry, I have no idea what you are talking about, can you get back to basics and start again*. This also breeds an introverted perspective, as they feel that to ask for help, advice or input on areas that they *think* they should already know is an admission of incompetence.

To get clients to really grasp this critical issue, I often explain the four stages of competency.

Conscious competency

Stage 1 – Unconscious incompetence

My daughter was three years old when I said, 'It's about time you knew how to tie your own shoelaces'. Up to that point she was unconsciously incompetent. That's to say that she didn't even know she couldn't tie her shoelaces because she didn't know she had to. She was blissfully unaware of her incompetence.

Stage 2 – Conscious incompetence

Of course, as soon as I mentioned it she became immediately consciously incompetent. Because I raised the issue, she suddenly became painfully aware of her incompetence.

Stage 3 – Conscious competence

Over the following days and weeks she learned that skill, and each time I talked her through it she gradually became consciously competent. That meant that if she thought carefully about the task in hand and blocked out other distractions, then she was now perfectly capable of tying her own laces.

Stage 4 – Unconsciously competent

Finally, after persevering for a few weeks she became unconsciously competent. She could now tie her laces without thinking and perhaps even while arguing about what she wanted for breakfast. It had become an automatic function that she could do without thinking.

The problem in many businesses is that the owners and managers are often unconsciously incompetent on some key issues. There are so many things that they don't know that they don't know. As soon as these issues are brought out into the open, they immediately become consciously incompetent.

Once the issue of conscious incompetence is raised, owners and managers become painfully aware of their limitations, the mistakes they have made along the way, some of their flawed decisions, and often how little they do know about running a business.

That is often a point where their enthusiasm drops, their energy levels go through the floor, and they want to throw in the towel – they have been caught out at last!

The reality is that nothing has changed!

Ouch!

Don't be afraid to get external input

My challenge as a coach and mentor is to make these key decision-makers understand that nothing has changed. Knowing what they didn't know has not actually changed their business at all. Although it often feels like a backward step to suddenly have a list of 100 things that should be done, in actual fact they have not moved at all, they have not gone backwards an inch. They do now at least have a good long list of actions that can and will help to drive their business forward. For many, ignorance is bliss, but if you really strive to have a successful business, and to be in a place where you feel completely competent to run it, then you need to go through the painful stage of being *consciously incompetent* and then *consciously competent* before you can reach the final stage. The issue of whether you become worse by knowing that there are some things you don't know is all in the mind.

Consider how you feel playing sport; perhaps golf, tennis or even chess. Whatever sport you do, or have played, you will no doubt have faced someone better than you and someone worse than you at some point. When you play against a better opponent you are much more aware of your limitations and their better skills. Play against someone who isn't quite as good, and you feel more confident and more in control. Your abilities are essentially the same in either scenario, but most people will benefit from playing someone better, as it helps them watch how things are done, pick up tips and techniques, and at the very least to see that it is possible to perform at that higher level. Your own performance may also improve in the face of the challenge although you may not enjoy it as much as you do beating someone not quite as good as you.

That's really business. You need to accept that you cannot know it all, and that there is always someone else who has skills, knowledge and experience to bring to the party. Even the very best sports players in the world have coaches, and many of these coaches could never have beaten the players they coach. It's about accepting that no one will think you are stupid for asking a question you don't know the answer to. Having met many business owners over the years, I can say that the least capable of them were not the ones that didn't know stuff, it was the ones that thought they already knew it all!

So whatever your role in your business, you need to come to terms with the fact that it is a constant learning experience. Open up to others about advice, guidance and support you may need, and put the hours in to learn the skills you need. Read books, use online research tools, go on courses and never be afraid to ask for help. Reading this book is a good place to start, but don't think that asking others to help implement the ideas in it is a sign of weakness or a lack of competence.

The key people in the profit equation

If you really want your business to succeed to its full potential, then you need to create an environment where everybody understands and accepts the need for constant development and improvement. Whether internal training courses, or external consulting advice, a culture that assumes you need to be better tomorrow than you are today is a crucial ingredient to success.

Bringing the issue back to *pricing for profit*, there are two main categories of people who are involved in issues that spring out of that subject. The first category includes the *decision-makers*. That may be a single owner/manager of their own business, or it may be a Board of Directors, including the CEO, Finance Director, Sales Director, HR Director, etc. It is essential that decision-makers are completely comfortable with the concept of continual improvement and development, and that the only constant in business is *change*. Nothing stands still and effort is needed to adapt and evolve to changing events. That may be recession, technology or personal issues such as funding limitations, etc. Decision-makers need to tackle pricing at a strategic level for their business.

In the context of pricing, these decision-makers need to drive the process of analysis, debate, agreement of action and implementation of change that will arise from working through all the Action Points in this book.

The second group who are essential to the implementation of pricing changes includes anyone on the *frontline*, handling pricing issues with customers. Across most businesses that includes:

- sales reps;
- account managers;
- counter staff;
- telesales;
- sales directors.

In some businesses that can include every single person in the business, who all muck in when needed.

Over many years working with businesses of all shapes and sizes, I have met just a handful of people who could be described as *professional* salespeople – meaning that they have had some element of training on selling skills, such as how to read body language, when to close the sale, how to negotiate, communication skills, presentation skills, etc. These great salespeople continually improve skills by reading books, listening to audio or watching video training programmes. They approach the sale professionally, preparing where possible, researching their customers, planning the sales approach, etc.

If you want to use pricing to grow profits, at some point you will need to deal with those people who are at the sharp end of delivering that message. These people need structure and guidance. They need motivating and managing and they need training and support. If you are serious about making your business more profitable, then invest some time and money in your frontline people.

When a customer says *that's a bit expensive* you need confidence that your people are ready for the question, trained on how to handle it, and that they have a number of options on how to balance the Value Scales, rather than apply a simple knee-jerk reaction and discount the price.

Let's look at a positive. It is human nature to want to please. Hopefully, all of your employees will have this natural desire to please the customers, as this is crucial to long-term success. Customers like dealing with nice people who are genuinely interested in helping them. The problem for businesses is that there are a variety of ways that these employees can please customers, and not all of them are good for business.

The cheapest way to make customers smile is to deliver exceptional customer service. We have all had examples of good and bad service and we have all felt first-hand the desire to spend more money and to return with future business, or conversely the desire to walk out, never return and to tell anyone who will listen how bad the service was.

My business partner and I had a great meal in a restaurant where we received truly exceptional service from a great waitress. She was enthusiastic and interested in the food on offer, listened to our preferences and guided us to what she suggested were the chef's specialities. It made us feel like we were the only ones she was looking after, and as a result we spent much more than we might otherwise have done. The prices of the food and drink became far less important because the experience was superb.

How much does it cost to deliver this exceptional service? Well, at a simplistic level, nothing at all. Manners and a smile cost nothing, as they say. Even at a practical level, the investment in better training, paying more than minimum wage, recruiting the right calibre of person, or having an extra person serving to ensure that everyone has the time to look after the customers, is still not a huge invest-ment compared to the returns. The principle is very simple. Happy customers spend more, and will pay more than unhappy ones. A restaurant offering only basic standards of food but delivered with exceptional service will do much better than one serving exceptional food with only basic service standards. People value feeling special and well looked after, and will pay for it in the price, or in higher spending (the extra bottle of wine or a dessert they might have skipped), or hopefully both.

The next way to make customers smile is to add increased value to the deal. Everyone likes to get something for nothing, and we all like to get a little extra we were not expecting. That may be as simple as a free trip to the salad bar in a restaurant, or it may be a bouquet of flowers left in the new car or by the estate agent when the house move goes through.

In most businesses adding value is an essential tool for making a sale happen by getting the Value Scales to tip towards the customer as was covered in great depth in Chapter 5. The principle is simple enough. If we have a string of options to add value to a sale and that have a comparatively low cost to us, we can make the customers smile.

The final option, and it should always be the last resort, is to reduce the price to improve the customer's perception of the value for money. The problem for most businesses is that this is often the *first* resort of the salesperson as it is the easiest way to make the customer that is standing right in front of them smile. The *real* pro-blem, however, is that every £1 knocked off the price is £1 straight off the bottom line profit.

As well as these two main categories, there is a third group of people who have an impact on the business through a variety of channels. There will be backroom staff who chase debts, deliver goods, handle phone calls or interact directly (and indirectly in the modern online business world we now occupy) with customers in all sorts of ways.

The key with this group is not much different from the objectives of the frontline group; ie making the experience of doing business with your organization as pleasant and as positive an experience as possible, in the knowledge that happy customers will spend more, pay more, and recommend your business to others.

Handling your team's need to please customers

Remember from earlier in the book, the guy named Derrick? He was the very popular salesperson who gave away huge discounts to make customers smile. The more discounts that he gave them, the bigger they smiled and the more often they came back to see him.

This story is repeated in many businesses across all sorts of industries. The natural human desire to please can be satisfied more easily and more quickly by dropping prices than it can be by upping your game on customer service or spending more time to explore any value-added options to put in to the deal. You need to make sure you give clear guidance on how your people can add value to your customers. Develop a long list of all the extras and add-ons that they can offer, and make sure that they understand the cost and value of each one. Of course, you must also set minimum standards of customer service, make sure the whole team stick to them, and continually seek to improve them. But above all else, make it hard for your people (and yourself if necessary) to give your money away. You can do this by limiting who is allowed to drop the price, to whom, when and why, and having a system that scores the cost of discounting prices between products, customers, branches and even individual salespeople. Re-read Chapter 10 if you are unsure on this issue.

Helping your team focus on profit

I have already mentioned that people are fundamentally lazy. They may not necessarily sit on their backsides all day unless kicked into action, just that they will be naturally drawn towards the *quick fix*, the *easy option* and the *simplest solution*. That may seem harsh, but who would deliberately choose the *hard option* or the *most complex solution*? What this usually means in the context of pricing is the use of a simplistic pricing model that makes life easier for the salesperson to handle. Again this is covered from different aspects throughout the book, but it is evident in situations such as:

- Offering 10 per cent, 20 per cent or 30 per cent discounts because they are easier to calculate than 16.58 per cent or 23.97 per cent, for example. Lazy salespeople jump too quickly to give 20 per cent off, when a little bit of effort might result in only 15.83 per cent, etc.

- Having all prices as a price for a single item and higher volumes as just a straight multiple of a single-unit price. Most businesses should offer multi-buy discounts or bundled deals to help increase the average value of each sale. But these different bundles need to be understood and explained by the salesperson, and that requires effort.

There is plenty of research that proves that the longer a salesperson spends with a customer, the higher the value of the sale. This requires taking the time to explore other products and services that the customer may want, and it should certainly include exploring the customer's perception of value. But it takes time to make the Value Scales tip by explaining the features and benefits more clearly, or by trying to add in extra value-added elements. It will almost certainly need some time spent explaining and justifying with confidence the price charged.

The temptation for many individuals – again simple human nature – is to get to the close quickly, get out and find another customer. In most cases the quickest way to close the sale is to lower your price until the customer is happy. Salespeople simply slash the price without dealing with any of the other options to make the Value Scales balance and the deal work.

Let's consider the issue from the other side. Your customers do not want to think that they have been taken for a ride, paying over the odds, or certainly not paying more than the next customer. None of us do.

Dealing with the human factor in your customers

Earlier chapters explored the way in which you discuss pricing issues with your customers, and how factors such as the way they pay will affect their decision-making. What customers want is an openness and directness to the pricing element of any sale. If they say *that seems expensive* they actually don't want to hear you say *OK, fine, I'll knock off 20 per cent*, as what this tells them is that you just tried to trick them out of an extra 20 per cent on the price. If your response is, 'Thank you for raising that point, can I just take a few moments to explain how we arrived at that figure so that you understand our prices?' that may well be all you need to do. If they still want a little more off the price, you may need to continue on with, 'But I may be able to look at a few things I could add in to make the deal a little better, if that helps you make a decision to buy from us today.' In most cases a clear, open and direct explanation is all that the customers want. Simple reassurance that the price you suggested was the *right* price, or a *fair* one.

There will be differences in the buying process depending on who you are dealing with. If you are dealing with a buying department, they will probably be better at negotiation than you are, and probably more focussed on the price having already excluded suppliers they don't believe are of the right quality or won't deliver in time. With these people you need to try and increase volumes for a lower price, and make sure payment terms are clear, etc. But don't think it is all about price. They may have important issues such as time of delivery, quality assurances or streamlined administration of your account. These often larger and more sophisticated clients understand the Value Scales issue, and although they may be tougher at getting what they want, pricing remains only one element of the deal. Being prepared is the key.

If you are dealing with someone simply tasked to spend company money on something such as more stationery, they may have been told to *get three quotes*, or *don't forget to ask for a discount*. You need to explore what they want, when they want it and perhaps explain to them why cheapest may not be best. It is often just a simple buying exercise where price is an automatic issue that you need to push to the back of their list in favour of all the other features and benefits of buying that product or service from you.

If it is an end consumer, then the same principles apply. A dialogue that covers the key issues of value and the features and benefits is essential. It may be a more direct issue as the money being spent is their own but, as covered in many previous chapters, very few of us buy the cheapest simply because it is the cheapest. We all want the best products and services at the lowest prices but we are all smart enough to know that dirt-cheap is rarely good.

Your frontline people need to think about the motivations of the customer, and in particular the individual they are dealing with. Very few customers are focussed on the lowest price at the exclusion of all other elements, and it is the frontline person's job to uncover the issue of most importance to each customer. Human nature will drive them to find the shortcut to a quick sale and you need to ensure that this doesn't happen, through training, better systems and some guidelines and rules on what they can and cannot do. Your sales people will scream that this is like asking them to juggle with one hand behind their backs – but even that can be done with three balls and practice!

Fear!

Let's tackle fear. The earlier example from DFAP, the tourist attraction, was an extreme reaction, where the owner wanted to reduce prices for more than 99,000 visitors in response to just 40 complaints. Countless times I have heard frontline people express this fear in a variety of ways; ie that they will lose the sale unless they are able to discount the price.

So how can you handle this problem?

First, it is really helpful to separate the person handling the reaction of the customer from the person making the decision on what action can be taken. When a client says *that's just too expensive, I want 20 per cent off,* and you have the power to make that decision there and then, the natural human desire to please can become a powerful emotion. The urge to fix it quickly and move on to the next sale probably means that you will go a long way, if not all the way to the 20 per cent reduction.

However, if you say something like, 'I'm sorry but that is the price that we have set for this work across the firm, to ensure all clients are treated fairly, so I cannot reduce the price just for you without discussing it first with a director' (or a manager or just a colleague), you have achieved a number of things. The customer will be reassured that the price is consistent with others and hence is 'fair' but, second, you have detached yourself from the issue by involving the other (not in the room) director. If the answer remains *no*, it is not you that is being stubborn or difficult, but the firm, or the system or the director. The most common reaction to the statement above is *OK, just thought I'd ask.*

A car salesperson was trying to sell a brand new car to his customer and was negotiating the value of the trade-in. He asked the customer what amount he was expecting, and was given quite a high figure for what they thought it was worth – £5,000. The salesperson was naturally concerned that if he couldn't agree a price for the trade-in, that he might lose the whole sale. So he listened to the customer's suggested trade-in value and then said that he wasn't authorized to make that decision so would need to go and check with a manager. He duly disappeared for five or six minutes. When he returned he said, 'I have really pushed my manager as far as I could, but he says that £3,000 is the fair price for the car.' He then said, in a slightly conspiratorial way, 'Look, I want to do this deal to hit my sales target, and I think I can push him up a little, tell me how low you would be prepared to go and I will see if I can beat that.' So the customer suggested that £4,000 was his bottom line.

The salesperson disappeared for a few more minutes and when he returned said, 'OK I managed to squeeze him up to £3,900 but that is absolutely as far as he would go.' They shook hands and did the paperwork.

What the salesperson did was to encourage the customer, in a clever way, to divulge their likely bottom end price, and to place the blame for the tough negotiation on a faceless manager. His fear of losing the sale may well have made the discussions with the customer difficult and encouraged him to give more on the trade-in than he had to. Instead, he made the customer believe that he was on their side and that someone else was taking the tough stance on the price. Did he really talk with a manager? Probably not, but even if he did, it would have been a well-rehearsed routine designed to have the effect that it did. By detaching the person at the sharp end of the discussion from the apparent decision on price it removes the salesperson's fear of losing the sale or of falling out with the customer.

It is natural for any of us to become defensive when talking about price, as any negotiation about it implies a criticism of the product or service we are seeking to supply. We also naturally want to avoid conflict, and as a result, when the person placed in the position of negotiating is also the person making the final decision on price, is it any wonder that they cave in too soon and give away too much. We allow the fear of losing the sale to directly affect the salesperson's decision-making. As with the detail in Chapter 10 on discounts, making frontline people seek authorization for discounts makes it much easier for them to say, *sorry, the manager says I can only go to x per cent*.

So look at the levels of authority that you allow your frontline people on the pricing issue, and see if you can add layers of authority that take the emotion away from the person doing the deal and allow them to build a better rapport with the customer. It is, of course, really important to acknowledge that the salespeople will fight you all the way on this, arguing that they need to have complete discretion to do the deal, and that having to check in with managers or directors for approval won't work. This is again a quite natural character trait that we all like to feel important, and adding in layers of authority for pricing or discounting decisions can make many frontline people feel less important. But trust me, it will actually make their lives easier and make the business more profitable.

Summary

Human beings are funny creatures. We often say one thing and mean another, and we have insecurities and idiosyncrasies that are hard to manage. As business owners and managers you will need to handle them very carefully in any area where you are implementing change and in particular to the emotive area of pricing.

If you want your business to be successful, there are some fundamentals of human behaviour you need to address. These include a desire to hide weaknesses, to avoid conflict, and to feel important.

You need to build a culture where there is an acceptance that no one ever knows it all, and that everyone can continue to develop and improve and, in fact, has an obligation to do so if they want to remain employed. In the context of pricing this means that the people at the top need to be much more open in debate and discussion on key issues and to think carefully how they make the decisions on pricing, and how they implement this with the people who have to apply those policies.

Taking the human factor out of the process, or limiting its impact by applying rules or forcing agreement from above on pricing decisions, will improve the overall prices and profits that you achieve.

Action points

1 Undertake a skills review of your key people (in the context of pricing that means the decision-makers and the frontline people) and assess their skills and experiences with regards to pricing, selling and customer-handling skills.

2 Get the Board/senior managers to self-assess their competency in following key business areas, and develop a training plan for each of them. These need only be short introductory courses of one or two days, which you should be able to source from local training providers:

   – understanding financial accounts;

   – managing and motivating people;

   – managing change;

   – leadership skills;

   – effective communication.

3 Continuing on, develop a training programme for all frontline people that includes:

- how to read body language;
- when to close the sale;
- how to negotiate;
- communication skills;
- telephone skills;
- presentation skills;
- basic financial understanding (mark-up vs margin, etc).

4 Get the pricing team to set discounting guidelines, and involve your HR team to design the rollout of training to sales managers and salespeople. Ideally, have the sales managers deliver the training to their people, so that culture change is built in and reinforced by those sales managers.

Getting financial clarity

14

It is perhaps inevitable that at least one chapter of the book is a numbers-based issue. As a qualified accountant these are familiar to me and easy to interpret and understand, but many business owners tremble at the thought of getting to grips with their *financials*.

This chapter will focus on just a handful of financial indicators to show where businesses fail to make the profits that they should and could make. Some points are about you understanding your own costs, others are about identifying true selling prices, and between the two falls the profit.

The vast majority of business owners and managers cannot properly read a set of financial statements. In truth they don't need to, but they should at least have some basic financial understanding of what a set of accounts tells them, and how various simple business actions impact profit. If a lawyer said *most clients don't really understand law* or a doctor said *most patients don't understand medicine* you wouldn't think it strange. The problem is that many people in business think that they *should* have some innate financial skill and are just too embarrassed to own up that they don't and to ask for help.

However, the intention here is not to embarrass anyone. If you are not naturally numerate, or you have concerns about your understanding of some of the financial implications of various actions suggested throughout the book, just find someone that is numerate and can help you get a grip on your numbers. The diagram in this chapter is intended to be a simple representation of the key issues, but for the non-financial reader it still may hold some challenges to truly understand. So if you don't get the points easily, share it with someone in your financial team and try to use numbers relevant to your own business and the issues should jump out at you. That may be your in-house bookkeeper or accountant, or it may be an external accountant.

This chapter includes:

- You need to know the numbers.
- Not all customers make you money.
- Steps in the profit calculation.

You need to know the numbers

The critical point for anyone involved in running a business is that if you want to increase its profits, then you will need to know your financial numbers to know what to do and to measure whether it has worked or not.

When working with business owners and managers to improve profits, there is often a point where a bold suggestion is made to the team in a business to address an issue. This may be something like, *discounting prices doesn't work, cutting prices by 10 per cent will need you to increase sales volumes by 50 per cent to make the same profit you used to make before the price drop*. Often someone will question that statement and want to see the maths proven. This is OK, and in fact it is much better than the alternative, which is that they don't agree but simply stay silent for the *fear of being caught out*.

Now, I can prove the maths. Chapter 10 addresses the madness of discounting and includes the great grid showing the impact of dropping prices at various different profit margins. The maths of every number on these diagrams is easy to calculate. A further example of this is below:

A business buys one style of trampolines at a cost of £200 and sells them at a price of £400, it is therefore making £200 profit or a 50 per cent margin. They sell 100 of these trampolines a year so turnover on this product is £40k, the total cost is £20k giving £20k profit at the 50 per cent margin.

If they cut their prices by 10 per cent, and sell the next 100 for only £360 each then the turnover reduces to £36k. However, the costs of these 100 items remain the same at £20k and the profit therefore drops to only £16k. Unless sales volumes do increase they have just lost £4k. Really, any result below the original £20k profit would make this a big mistake, so the question is, how many more do they need to sell to get back to where they were?

To get the profit back up to £20k they need to make another £4k profit, and at the new prices that will be 25 more trampolines; ie the price of £360 each, less cost of £200 equals £160 profit. So £4,000 divided by £160 requires 25 more units to get back to where they started. That means 125 units to achieve the same result as before.

If you are running any business, you need to consider these numbers for each one of the products or services you sell. If you drop the prices by £x on item A, how much more of it do you need to sell to get back to where you started? Or if you raise the price of item B by x per cent how much volume can you afford to lose before you are worse off? These numbers are not *experiences*, or *judgements*, they are mathematical facts.

As a business decision-maker, you are then required to make a subjective judgement of whether these calculated volume changes are *likely* to happen with an increase or fall in price, but that is a judgement based on the financial facts, *not* a judgement based on guesswork.

Many salespeople will say something along the lines of *if we drop prices by 10 per cent we will sell more and be better off*. An *instinctive judgement* but without financial facts. If we are able to establish the facts (say):

- Current sales volumes 100 units pa
- Cost £200 each

- Price £400 each

- Margin 50 per cent or £200 profit per unit.

We can then calculate that a planned 10 per cent price drop reduces the margin to only £160 per unit, and that we will need to sell 25 extra units to get back to where we started. Then the only subjective judgement is whether selling 10 per cent cheaper will lead to increased sales volumes of an extra 25 per cent.

What every business needs to do is to establish facts and limit the areas of subjective judgement or instinct. In most cases the reality becomes obvious; ie in the example above, it is very common that in the absence of facts a decision would have been made to drop the prices based on the broad assumption that volumes would increase and so would profits. But as soon as the reality of needing a 25 per cent jump in volumes has been calculated, not even the most optimistic salesperson would think it was a smart move. Even if they did, then that becomes a clear and measurable target for the salesperson; ie if you want to drop the price by 10 per cent, then you *need* to deliver a 25 per cent improvement in volumes. Good luck!

Not all customers make you money

Chapter 8 had a section entitled *every customer is worth having and every sale matters*. This considered the idea that most businesses have a wide range of customers they serve, from the regular, high-spending, quality customers who appreciate value for money and are prepared to pay the prices that you ask, right down to the low-spending, once in a blue moon, always-complaining variety.

It explored the idea of trying to determine a value for each customer served, whether based on spending, profitability, or even just the hassle factor of dealing with them. You then need to decide the point at which it is just not economic to deal with a customer; ie a highly demanding customer that generates a low profit may not be worth the hassle and cost for the small profit you earn. Armed with this data showing a value for each customer and having determined the line below which you are probably losing money, it is a simple exercise of listing the customers and seeing who is below that line.

Once again there is subjectivity to the assessment that the decision-makers in the business need to apply, but the details in Chapter 8 show that most businesses lose money on the bottom end of their customer list. This is a little easier in business-to-business organizations with account customers, as the history of transactions is clearer to see customer by customer. However, the logic applies to retail businesses as well, it is just harder to make some of the judgements when customers are to a great extent anonymous. Even in these businesses we need to try and segment groups of customers into frequent high spenders, frequent low spenders, occasional high spenders and occasional low spenders. We then aim to get the low spenders spending more each time and the occasional customers spending more often. Without this data, it is very hard to develop and implement any specific strategy to improve.

In the B2B businesses where the information is more readily available it is just a question of determining and applying some rules that encourage the poor-quality customers to spend more, pay more, or to leave. This can be done by setting prices higher at the start, or by restricting discount percentages or the situations in which they apply. Some businesses have implemented retrospective discount policies so that customers only get their 20 per cent off after they have purchased, *and paid for*, £1,000 worth of goods (or whatever level they set in their organization).

A number of retail businesses have created a variation of a membership scheme (not quite as grand as the Tesco Clubcard but the same idea) where they promise customers who join special deals. Some of these deals are special prices on bundles of products, some are access to training and demonstration events, or perhaps free delivery on spending above £x. Although often done more as a marketing tool than a customer segmentation device, this has a number of benefits. First, it gives you the details of what were previously anonymous customers – email addresses, decision-makers' names, etc – that help you build a history of spending from that customer in future. It also gives you a direct list of customers to whom you can promote special deals.

One such business is a large chain of butchers. They have 99 per cent retail customers who walk into any one of their stores to buy fresh meat and related products. They developed a membership club called *The Ruby Club*, which now has 14,000 members on the database. The company can track spending habits, promote specials offers and prompt with ideas for summer barbecues, Easter, Christmas and Valentine's meals and much more. Every time they send an email there is a definite spike in sales for the items being promoted.

How does a members club apply to price? What this enables the business to do is to generally raise prices for all customers, so that all of the infrequent, small-spending customers may pay, say, 4 per cent or 5 per cent more on what they buy. Members then get access to special prices through their membership, which brings them back down to the original prices, or if they spend enough, slightly below. The idea is that you don't give automatic discounts to everyone (by virtue of generally lower prices) but only to those customers who earn it. Building membership arrangements allows retail businesses to achieve this.

If a non-member complains about the price, the answer is simple – join the club if you want the best deals. This allows the owner to continually prompt for extra business, and continue to build knowledge and data on its customer base.

The problem is real, and almost certainly applies in your business. You lose money on probably the bottom 25 per cent of your customers because the profit from that occasional, low-value sale just isn't enough to cover the true costs of doing that transaction.

So if you are in a B2B type of operation, do the numbers and set a point below which it is uneconomic to do business. Anyone below that is looked at to either increase the price or to increase the volumes to get them above the line, or they are encouraged to go elsewhere.

In a retail or B2C business, you still need to try and adopt the same mentality that a section of your customer base loses you money each time they do business with you. If they are anonymous, that is hard to deal with, so why not capture their details in some form of members club. Failing that, put prices up and offer discounts only when a customer spends more than £x.

Steps in the profit calculation

The series of diagrams below shows the differences between the profits businesses think (or pretend) they are making, and the profits they actually make. It also looks at the profit they could make if they had the confidence to charge what they are really worth, or perhaps even to improve the quality or features of what they currently offer to their customers. It is complicated so we will take it one step at a time.

It charts a line that could be the price of any product or service. As the price 'P' increases towards the maximum price, the profit 'X' will also increase.

FIGURE 14.1

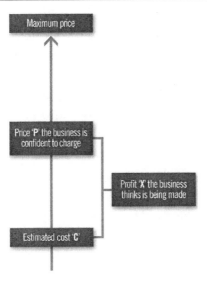

The starting point on the diagram is *estimated cost* 'C', which is what the business has assessed as the *cost* of buying or producing what it is that they sell. The second number is the *price* 'P' that the business is currently confident to charge, which is the overall sales value that it *thinks* it achieves from its transactions with customers. The difference between these two is therefore the profit 'X' that the business *thinks* is being made. We will address the *thinks* point later.

Therefore if the business had an estimated cost 'C' of an item at £75, and sold at a price 'P' of £100, then they would be making a profit 'X' of £25 and a margin of 25 per cent. Simple.

For any business it is therefore essential to ensure that we sell at a price above cost, otherwise we are making a loss. I know that is obvious, but you would be amazed how many businesses don't manage to do this. Some, to be fair, make the mistake by accident, while others actually do it deliberately.

To truly understand the profit equation better we need to analyse the numbers in a little more depth:

Let's look at those businesses that sell at a loss by accident.

If you are in a business where you buy in an item, let's say a new car for £18,000, then you know exactly the cost and that you need to sell for a price of at least £18,001 to make a profit. But what if you do not buy the car, but instead you manufacture it from raw materials, or perhaps you are in a business that provides knowledge, experience or just time. How do you work out the cost then?

In a good business you should still know the cost of what you sell by monitoring the costs of each element of the process – the raw materials, use of machine time, labour hours, etc – and having the accountant work out how overheads and other expenses should be shared over the products made. Sadly, very few owner-managed businesses have this level of financial control and are therefore working *in the dark* as to the true cost of the product or service they sell. If that is you, then you need to get your advisers involved and work out accurately your true cost.

Even if you are able to accurately identify the basic cost of what you sell, many businesses still underestimate the peripheral costs of serving each customer. One large business uses the term *cost to serve*. They quantified the additional costs of getting stock in to the business (purchasing department salaries, delivery costs, etc), the cost of holding the stock on the shelf (insurance, funding, wastage, pilfering, warehouse rent, etc) and the costs of selling and delivering (counter staff wages, delivery costs, etc). Finally, an often-missed area is the cost of waiting to be paid (funding, debt collection costs, postage for statements and bad debts, etc). Their calculations suggested that there was a big difference between the estimated cost 'C' that they normally considered, and the true cost 'T' (see diagram below) of the sale. On average the true cost was 5.8 per cent higher than the estimated cost. Whatever the calculation or the terminology you use, the key point is that the cost of the item is not the only cost you incur to do that deal.

FIGURE 14.2

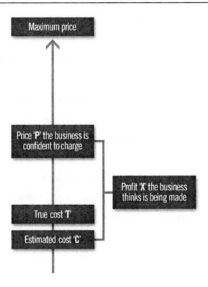

The diagram now shows this true cost 'T', which is always slightly, or sometimes a lot, higher than the estimated cost 'C' that the business was using to work out its profit. When you know this number you will almost certainly find some products and some customers where the profit margin doesn't cover these extra costs. In the example above they concluded that the true cost of items was 5.8 per cent higher than the estimated cost, but some frontline people were doing deals at 5 per cent margins in the belief that this was still profitable business.

So knowing accurately the true cost of what you sell is a critical start point.

It is entirely understandable that businesses that do not have this information may sell at a price that does not reflect the true cost. If challenged by a customer the salespeople may lack the confidence to stand their ground as it may appear to both the salesperson *and* the customer that the business is making more profit than it actually is.

The answer for this group of businesses who are *mistakenly* selling at a loss is to get better financial information to calculate their true cost and ensure that every sale is really generating profit. Many businesses now enter the cost onto the computer systems as the amount they actually pay to buy the item, and then add a standard uplift of, say, 5 per cent or 10 per cent to reflect an educated guess for all the peripheral expenses of handling whatever it is that the business sells. This is a simple approach that you could adopt immediately with little difficulty.

But what of those selling at a loss deliberately?

Covered in great depth in Chapter 8, the key issue is that some business owners and decision-makers genuinely believe that selling product A at a loss can be justified as it then results in selling more of products B, C and D, for example. It very rarely does and is a strategy that must be very carefully considered before being adopted.

In terms of the diagram, the key issue is that the estimated cost is very often lower than the true cost, and as a result the business isn't making as much profit as it thinks it is.

More about this shortly, but for the moment let's consider the price the business is confident to charge.

This should be a simple area, as most businesses at least know what they are charging their customers. However, I have seen countless businesses where I ask the owners, CEO, directors, etc, what the price of various items are, and their understanding is quite different from reality! This is occasionally where prices have crept up and the decision-makers are out of date, but more often than not it is that prices have been eroded over time and various products and services are being sold at less than expected.

However, there is normally some clarity that the business has a set of prices that are understood and broadly used, based on what it thinks it can reasonably charge in the marketplace. If you don't have that clarity, then you really need to get it. If you have a business where no one really knows what the prices should be and as a result frontline people are using *best guesses*, *judgement*, *instinct* or any other random determination of what they will charge, then you really do need more structure and control.

The key point to be understood is the price *actually* charged. Once again, other chapters have explored this area in more detail and looked into aspects such as discounting to make the sale, early settlement discounts to prompt faster payment and a number of other 'adjustments' that reduce the price quoted or published to the actual price achieved 'A'.

FIGURE 14.3

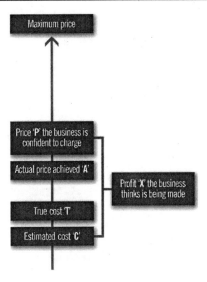

This is where many businesses go wrong. They use figures they believe are correct, but which just aren't.

One business identified the price they had set for more than 5,000 items that they sold. For each one they established the true cost, and the average discount that had been given over the previous financial year. They were astounded to see that on more than a quarter of these items they were giving more discount than the margin they were expecting to make, and as a result they were actually selling them at a loss.

What you can now see after placing the boxes for the true cost 'T' and the actual price achieved 'A' on to the diagram, is that the

FIGURE 14.4

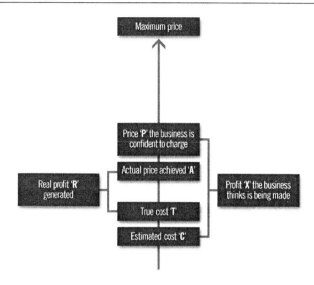

business is not making the profit 'X' that it thinks it is. The real profit 'R' is always less than the business expects.

Let's put some numbers on this to make it clearer:

- Estimated cost 'C' £75
- True cost 'T' £80
- Price 'P' the business is confident to charge £100
- Actual price achieved 'A' £95

Using these numbers we can see that the business thinks it is making a profit 'X' of £25 on £100 of sales, or a 25 per cent margin, when in fact it is only making a real profit 'R' of £15 on £95 of sales or just 15.8 per cent. That means they are making £10 less profit than they thought they were.

In many businesses the difference between the price 'P' a business thinks it is achieving and the actual price achieved 'A' that it does get, can easily be as much as 20 per cent, and the difference between the estimated cost 'C' and the true cost 'T' can easily be 10 per cent.

The key is that if you are 20 per cent lower on price than you think, and 10 per cent higher on cost, the difference between the profit 'X' you think you are making and the real profit 'R' that you actually make, can be absolutely huge. You need to know these numbers.

There are a couple of further elements to consider.

Real value

Throughout the book we have talked about the idea of a scientifically calculated price that reflects the real value the customer gets from any product or service. This is a combination of the benefits that they get from the item, alternative prices of competitors, the cost of substitutes, etc. Let's just say that this is the price that you would charge if you were able to read the mind of the customer to see how much they would really be willing to pay you.

Clearly it is not possible to look up this figure in a book, or even create any formula yourself. The only way to establish the real value of what you deliver to your customers is a process of trial and error and of elimination to get to the point where customers stop buying and go elsewhere. You can, of course, ask them for this information, and you will get some useful feedback, but rarely will a customer tell you the maximum price they will pay. That is your job or the job of your sales force to determine, by testing the prices, pushing the boundaries and carefully handling the situations where you hit the point where customers react.

There is almost always a huge gap between the actual price achieved 'A' by any business and the real value 'V' that they deliver to their customers. This is shown on the next diagram as the *confidence gap* 'G'. This is because it simply arises from the business's lack of confidence to charge the maximum price that it can.

Earlier chapters have covered this ground, but it is essentially the fear of what might happen if a business sets its prices too high that prevents them from pushing the boundaries and squeezing their prices up. Obviously every penny lost in this confidence gap would otherwise go straight to the bottom line of profit as there are no costs associated with getting this extra revenue.

A great strategy for many businesses is to simply try to ease up the price by very small increments on the basis that it just eats into this

FIGURE 14.5

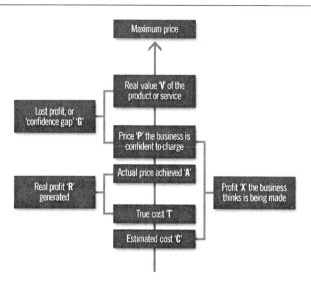

confidence gap and will therefore have no impact on the volume of sales or even the satisfaction of customers.

There are a number of different ways to gradually try to ease up the price, many of which are covered in earlier chapters. The basic point is that very small changes that are well explained simply do not affect the customer's appreciation of value.

Many business owners, having resisted the idea and made all sorts of excuses, have been amazed at the total lack of response from customers once they were eventually persuaded to have a go and stick the price up. The confidence gap is often 10 per cent, 20 per cent or even over 30 per cent of turnover, and to ease up the prices by 2 per cent, 3 per cent or even 5 per cent quite often doesn't register with the majority of customers.

The staggering part is the potential profit increases that can be achieved.

Take a modest business turning over just £500k pa. It has a cost of sales of say £350k and overheads of another £100k, leaving just £50k profit on the bottom line.

If the confidence gap is 10 per cent, 20 per cent or even 30 per cent, then they may be able to easily get away with a price increase of, say,

5 per cent with no impact on volume of sales or even triggering any kind of customer reaction at all. If they could, then all of this price increase would go onto turnover adding £25k, with no change to the Costs, therefore adding £25k straight to profit. This represents a 50 per cent uplift!

But what if the business could get the entire confidence gap? If it were 30 per cent, this would add £150k to profits, in effect quadrupling them. I have seen many businesses that have achieved this kind of dramatic impact on the profit, and some of these businesses would perhaps not even still be here if they hadn't implemented the changes!

Maximum price

Is this the end of the line? If they have got their price as close as possible to the real value then is that as far as a business can go?

No.

The final level is to try and move the real value as far as possible to achieve the maximum price possible for the goods and services being provided.

There are very few businesses that could not improve their customer service levels. If we work on all the possible aspects where we can improve what we do, then we may be able to move the value we deliver further. This may include direct customer service issues such as the way we answer the phone and the way we meet and greet customers who walk in. But it also extends to the after-sales processes, such as how we collect the money and how we deal with problems.

My favourite is the idea of the *free return ticket* that we put in place at the tourist attraction. In outline we put the gate prices up by over 20 per cent and wanted to add some value to justify it. We did this in part by offering the visitors free return entry as many times as they wanted within the next seven days. Obviously we had moved the real value up significantly by allowing in effect seven entries for the price of one, getting as close as we can to the maximum price that we could achieve. These returning visitors then spent money on food, drinks, ice creams, souvenirs, etc, because their subsequent visits were *free*, so that the average spend per head also increased.

Summary

What this chapter explores is the basic logic that only selling at a price above the cost of an item will generate a profit. CEOs, directors, business owners and managers will know this already.

In considering this simple sum it also looks at the problem that many businesses are working with inaccurate figures for cost, and inflated expectations of the price they will actually achieve, and you can see how wrong decisions get made.

Let's call the difference between the profit 'X' the business thinks is being made, and the real profit 'R' generated, the *expectation gap*. In the simple example earlier this was the difference between the profit they *expected* to achieve of £25 and the profit they *actually* made of £15. In some ways it is nothing more than a wake-up call to explain to those who need to know, why the profit is lower than expected. However, as soon as you identify the reasons why your true costs are slightly higher than your estimated costs, or why your actual price achieved is lower than the price you thought you were charging, then you have a chance to work on reducing the gap. Once again the significance of knowledge is explained simply as:

> What you can measure you can manage, and what you can manage you can improve.

You need to have accuracy in the financial information you use to make the right pricing and other decisions in your business.

It isn't as simple as this, though, as we also need to consider the gap between the *value* that these decision-makers place on what they sell – the price they charge – and the *value* that the customers may actually place on it. Fix this and there is potential to squeeze profits up even further. This *under-pricing* is down to a lack of courage to charge what the product or service is really worth, and this is why it is referred to as the confidence gap.

What you need to do is to find ways of establishing the size of the expectation gap and the confidence gap, and then use the other chapters in this book to identify ways to reduce them.

Only you can determine whether you are sufficiently numerate, or have the right resources on your team, but if you don't, then find external input to get the clarity that you need.

Action points

1 Share the diagram with your pricing team and ensure that everyone understands the potential causes of the expectation gap, and the confidence gap.

2 Get the pricing team to do a review of your top 10 products or services and get them to consider the key elements of the diagram in relation to these; ie:

   – What is the estimated cost 'C' for the item and how does this differ from the true cost 'T'?

   – Where do these extra costs arise and how are they incurred and controlled?

   – Quantify the difference between the price 'P' being charged and the actual price achieved 'A'.

   – If discounts are a key cause, refer to all the actions in the chapter on that topic, or identify the other factors creating this variance.

3 Based on the information generated in 2, ask the pricing team to develop and implement a plan to manage and reduce the impact of these issues on your profit margin.

4 Ask the pricing team to undertake some customer research to try and establish the potential magnitude of the confidence gap. This could include:

   – A generic customer survey of a selection of clients, part of which asks for an indication of the value being delivered on a scale of 1 to 10. Scores consistently at 7 or above would indicate that customers' perception of value is high and that you may be able to move prices up.

- Run a Customer Advisory Board. This gets a key group of important customers into a room to discuss various aspects of what you do and what they would like you to do. It can ask for feedback on customer service and product range as well as their perception of how the Value Scales currently look.

- Test some changes on clients who you are comfortable may opt to leave; ie ones below the line where it is economic to do business with them.

5 Based on your findings in 4, ask the pricing team to develop changes to your current pricing strategy to seek to close the confidence gap.

6 To help you get some enthusiasm for the work, calculate what the impact would be on your bottom line of addressing these issues; ie what would be the improvement in your bottom line profit if you were able to raise prices and lose no customers at all, using, say, 1 per cent, 2 per cent, 5 per cent and 10 per cent increases?

Using the earlier example of a £500k turnover business making £25k on the bottom line, the results would be:

Price increase	Impact on turnover and profit	Per cent growth in profit
1 per cent	£5,000	20
2 per cent	£10,000	40
5 per cent	£25,000	100
10 per cent	£50,000	200

Download the iPad App to explore these issues for your business.

Your action plan 15

There are hundreds of good ideas in this book that work. There are thousands more that you could get from reading other books or from just a simple Google search. Getting knowledge on this business-critical topic of pricing is the easy bit.

Implementing change is the only thing that will improve your bottom line profit.

Whatever your role in your business – CEO, director, owner, manager or simply an employee wanting to develop and progress – you need to develop an action plan for change, and you will at some stage need to engage the energy and enthusiasm of others above, below or alongside you.

There are some key steps in achieving any change in business. This chapter seeks to help you implement changes and improvements to the area of pricing, but many of the principles apply to any change management process.

In this chapter you will see how to:

- Have a vision for the future.
- Build your team and allocate resources.
- Set SMART goals.
- Just do stuff!

Have a vision for the future

Be honest about this: pricing is an emotive issue, and you will almost certainly encounter some resistance to any changes you make. However, it is important to understand that this resistance is just as likely to come from within your business as it is to come from your customers.

Therefore, getting key people in your organization on board with the objective of increasing profits through better pricing skills is crucial. A great starting place is to quantify the potential profit improvements from relatively small changes in key areas.

If you wish to use it, an iPad App has been developed so that you can play with your existing business's financial performance by looking at a number of *what if* scenarios. The ideas behind this were covered very early on in Chapter 1, but the App just simplifies the calculations to make the impact easier to see.

Whether you use the simplistic models discussed in this chapter's Action Points, or download the App, what you will undoubtedly see is that the greatest and easiest impact on profits will come from getting better at pricing. So if you personally need the motivation to change, or are seeking to enthuse others, do the calculations and see what the impact could be for your business. It is very common to achieve at least a 1 per cent or 2 per cent improvement in profit margins, which often has the impact of doubling bottom line profits, and many businesses achieve profit margin increases of 5 per cent to 10 per cent. See what your profitability could be if you get these changes right.

It is a basic human characteristic that people need to be motivated to change, or punished for resisting it. Simple *carrot and stick*. When you know the numbers, why not put some of the potential improvement on the table as a reward for the pricing team doing the analysis and implementation, for the sales team in adapting their approach, or the whole team for playing ball with the changes you adopt. It can be a fixed percentage of the uplift in profits, or a fixed sum to be shared out only if profit margins improve by x per cent. Let them see how the changes will benefit them and change will be much easier.

If it is your business and you will be doing all of the hard work, why not commit to booking that great holiday you can never quite justify if you improve margins by x per cent in the next six months?

The basic logic is obvious. Everyone, including you, is more likely to embrace the ideas and work hard to achieve the improvements if there is something in it for them, and you need to paint a clear picture of what the future could be like if you get it right.

Build your team and allocate resources

Throughout the book I have referred to the pricing team. If your business is large enough, this should include senior people from the sales and marketing sides of the business, as these are the people who will have to adapt the outward messages for your customers and your marketplace, and deliver the changes in pricing that you decide. It should also include people from your finance team so that you have someone detached from the frontline who can simply work out the maths of the various actions and ideas you may seek to implement.

As many chapters have already discussed, a big part of the problem for many organizations is that the people in charge of setting prices or reducing them by discounts are those at the sharp end who develop a fear of bad customer reactions, or who lack the numeracy to understand the financial impact of what you need to change. So get numbers people into the team.

Regardless of your size, the ideas in the book will also require training of those affected by the changes, and management of change itself. People naturally fear any change, as they are uncertain of what this will mean for them, and they are fearful of getting things wrong. If you have an HR department, get them involved to ensure people are comfortable with what is happening, are guided through the implementation of the ideas, and have a route to raise concerns if they want to. The HR team can also then work on sourcing training, or creating the in-house training that will be needed for the frontline team and perhaps others.

Regardless of whether your team is 8 to 10 people or just you and one other, you need to make sure that they have the time and resources to undertake the work properly. That will mean allocating time on a regular basis for them to meet, debate issues, analyse information and agree actions. It will also mean that they will need to do work during their normal week that could interfere with their normal day jobs.

In many change management projects the failures result from the fact that responsibilities and pressures are added to the workload of busy people, and either never gets done, or is done in a rush with far less attention than it deserves.

If you have done the first part of this chapter and calculated the potential profit improvement your business could achieve, you should have the confidence to ensure that work on this topic is high up the pricing team's priority list and gets done. If this is a problem, then you may need to consider giving these people additional resources (part-time assistants, etc) to free up their time.

As with all teams, it needs leadership. If you are the CEO or business owner, then that may be you, or you may delegate it to someone else to run. What is often a serious problem in these situations is to have someone who is immersed in the detail also seeking to lead the project. If you are able, have someone that understands the objectives and is respected by the team, but who can keep away from the day-to-day actions, to lead the project.

The final aspect of building the right pricing team is to consider the inclusion of outsiders. Inevitably those within your business have a different perspective on it than those outside of it. Your team may be more emotive about issues than someone who doesn't have the responsibility of implementing any changes, and they may also bring other skills and experiences of similar businesses or even direct competitors.

You could consider the following:

- customers – even if included for only some aspects;
- suppliers;
- similar businesses from different areas where you may share knowledge;
- your accountant;
- a business friend or contact;
- external consultants;
- university graduates on an internship.

Set smart goals

If you want to make any changes, then you need to be crystal clear what these are, how they will be achieved and when they will be done. Just saying *we will improve our profit margins* is not enough, otherwise you will look back at any improvement and regard it as a great success. Say how much you want them to improve, and by when that should be achieved. It won't matter if you miss, but you are significantly more likely to get a better result if you set clear, unambiguous targets.

Whatever actions you choose to take, set a deadline for action, and divide this into milestones so that you can measure progress along the way and monitor whether you are on track or not.

You may well have seen it before, but the acronym SMART is still very important in setting any goals. There are a number of variations of it, but consider:

S – Specific. Clear to everyone involved in the project.

M – Measurable. *2 per cent increase* in margins rather than just *an improvement.*

A – Agreed upon. You will not achieve goals if some team members are resisting you.

R – Realistic. Within your resources and time constraints.

T – Time based. State when you aim to hit the various goals set.

Just do stuff!

Writing with a passion about pricing has been easy, and a lot of effort has gone into writing Action Points for the end of each chapter. However, those were designed to get you thinking about particular issues raised within that chapter. What follows now has a slightly different emphasis. There are 42 Action Points that are presented a little more forcefully – just get on and do these things, starting right now.

The order is not important, with the single exception of Number 1 (put your prices up by 5 per cent right now). Read them all, tick 14, then just do this stuff!

1 Just put your prices up right now

- Add 5 per cent to everything, effective at the start of next month.

- Develop a short role-play training module that shows the salespeople how to handle the objections that may be raised by customers. It should also address how to deal with any who decide to stop buying from you (so that they don't bad-mouth your business in the marketplace).

- If it is absolutely necessary for you to include a safety net for any particularly difficult customers who are critical to the ongoing success of your business, then begin by finding creative ways to increase the value you deliver to those customers. Agreeing to any special discounts for them should be a last resort, and you should still aim to achieve at least a 2.5 per cent increase.

- For larger businesses with many branches, you may be tempted to try this 5 per cent increase in just one branch as a trial. If so, follow this guidance to maximize the necessary culture change:

  a Select a pilot branch. This should be the one that has your best sales team.

  b Have a training provider and sales manager write down the approach you will use.

  c Use the trainer and sales manager to jointly train the team.

  d Set up the salespeople to roll out the 5 per cent increase, starting with their C-grade customers and building up to the A-grade ones.

  e Stop after each customer category to discuss and review the outcomes.

  f Once the roll-out has finished, have your finance people assess the *before* and *after* profitability of that branch.

g Adapt the training to use over all remaining branches.

h Prepare a programme to implement the 5 per cent price increase over all branches.

i Use the sales manager and salespeople from the pilot branch to deliver training to the other branches.

2 Know your numbers

- Which 10 customers contribute the most to turnover?
- Which 10 customers contribute most profit?
- Which 20 products generate the highest gross profit?
- Which 20 products generate the highest gross profit percentage?
- Who are your top salespeople?
- Which branches yield the greatest profit?
- Which sales channels (retail, online, etc) generate the greatest profit?

Let other people gather their detailed reports, but if you are the person at the top of your business, you need this *whole-of-business* profit summary, updated monthly. Keeping this information at your fingertips sends the strongest signal ever that you are fully focused on profits.

3 Invest some time on the issue

- Appoint a pricing team, made up of just a few people; one must be a finance person and one must be a seasoned face-to-face salesperson.
- Assign a single person to be the leader of that team.
- At their first meeting, empower them to gather data, analyse it, argue and debate, negotiate points of view and present back to you robust pricing strategies and critical actions for the business.

This team's first review will take some effort, but after that you want a review submitted every quarter.

4 Don't let your salespeople set the price

- The pricing team will present pricing strategies and discounting guidelines that protect and improve profits. Don't allow frontline people to overrule this.

- The strategies and guidelines will likely be high level, so this must be translated into information, procedures and training of frontline salespeople. If your organization is large, this can be left to the sales department. If your business is small, the pricing team can do this.

You can expect resistance from salespeople, so in larger businesses you should consider engaging a change management expert to assist in this process. In a smaller business make it crystal clear that you expect your people to raise issues properly and accept the changes that you decide.

5 Not every customer is worth having

- Analyse your customers in order of the profit they generate for your business. Mark the top 10 per cent as A-grade customers; the next 60 per cent as B-grade; the following 10 per cent are C-grade.

- Look carefully at the bottom 20 per cent. By involving the salespeople and a simple and subjective show of hands, mark those that are *easy to deal with*, and those who are a *pain*.

- Take action. The customers who are a 'pain' should be sacked. The others should have their prices adjusted upwards, so that you can try to nudge them into the C-grade category.

6 Train your salespeople to understand the financial dynamics of business

- Develop a short training module that addresses the impact of price discounting, and the merits of losing some customers to get a higher price from others (Chapter 10). This can be written in-house if you have the resources, or you can use a local training organization.

- Train your sales managers first, and then have those managers deliver the module to their salespeople. This is an important part of achieving culture change.

7 Limit discounts

- Ask the pricing team to set clear and fixed discount limits.
- Have the team write guidelines that address customers who are out of normal credit terms, forfeiting the right to discounts. Also, customers who spend less than £x a year and therefore should not qualify for special prices.
- Ask salespeople to report monthly on any discounts given outside of the guidelines and to justify why they gave it; eg to price-match a competitor. Insist upon evidence to prove it, such as a copy of the competitor's quote.

8 Score discounts

- Have your finance people report monthly on the 'loss' of income caused by discounts being given. Ideally, they should set up an automatic reporting system so that this happens easily.

9 Manage discounts

- Monitor the discounts being given by each salesperson and provide training to any who are giving away too much of your money.
- Monitor the discounts being given by each branch and address this issue directly with the branch manager.
- Monitor the discounts on each product and assess the reason for excessive amounts, and whether that product should still be sold.
- Monitor the discounts to each customer and consider whether their categorization (A–C) is correct. If not, review their viability as an ongoing customer.

10 Don't rely on anecdotal evidence of what others are charging

- Have the sales managers establish a file on their main competitors, and include a file on their own branch.

- The files should contain brochures, price lists and any other hard evidence that can be summarized into a value statement for each competitor.

- Ask the pricing team to analyse the information – looking for every opportunity to adjust your own prices upwards – and then make recommendations to you. Their recommendations should include a Profit Impact estimate.

- Build in to your systems that the sales managers continually update the files.

11 Don't use round sum prices

- Adjust all of your prices to non-round figures; eg change a £100 price upwards to, say, £101.87.

12 Loss leaders don't work

- Have your pricing team work closely with the sales manager(s) to list all loss leaders – those products and services that are being used as a deliberate strategy to get footfall.

- Get your finance people to work out the numbers.

- Ask your finance people to calculate the profit impact of immediately lifting the prices of all loss leaders to a level consistent with all other pricing.

- Increase those prices.

- If your business has many branches and you want to run a pilot, pick a branch where the sales manager and salespeople are known to be keen supporters of change. Measure their results and develop a case study to aid the roll out across every branch.

13 Don't give anything away for free

- Study the components of your value offer to customers and identify every instance where you give something for free. This could be a free consultation, free servicing, free training, free delivery, etc.

- Apply a published value to those elements, and then design a way that the customer still gets this value 'for free'. Two examples:

  - *Delivery is £8.97, but as a special deal for you/the first 100 customers/this month there will be no charge, saving you £8.97.*

  - *Initial consultations are £242 per hour, but our policy is not to charge for the first 1-hour appointment.*

14 Re-word prices for increased perception of value

- Identify all bland descriptions of price; eg *price is £2,000*.

- Re-word these such that the perception of value is emphasized. For example:

  - The price of the fitted bedroom is £2,000; becomes

  - Your *investment* in a *fabulous new* fitted bedroom is *only* £2,000.

15 Re-word prices for relativity

- Identify all 'raw' price tags; eg £102.48.

- Have your marketing people re-word all tags, banners, brochures and catalogues such that a perception of relativity is presented. Examples:

  - *Half price at £102.48*

  - *Manager's deal of the week £102.48*

  - *End-of-season price £102.48*

  - *Limited offer at £102.48.*

16 Prepare your salespeople to defend prices with confidence

- Set up a short-term project team of your best salespeople. Ask them to develop a short role-play training module on how a salesperson should respond to the question, *That price seems expensive, can you knock something off?*

- Ensure that this becomes mandatory training for all employees who interact with the customers.

- Require that this training is completed within three months from today.

17 Explore ways to add value to your offer

- Set up a short-term project team of your best marketing and salespeople. Ideally these might be new recruits who have worked in similar roles in different industries.

- Ask them to develop fresh ways of adding value to your offer. One source would be the competitor files mentioned earlier. By adopting and adapting one good idea from each of five competitors, your business will leapfrog all five.

- They should also brainstorm new ideas with an external facilitator.

- Accept the recommendations and ask the pricing team to design a roll-out plan, with appropriate supporting documents (eg brochures) and an accompanying training strategy to ensure that salespeople are skilled at communicating the increased value offers to their customers.

18 Look for partnership deals

- Set up a short-term project team of your most connected marketing and salespeople to investigate partnership deals that would be of mutual benefit. For example:

  - A wedding photographer could offer deals that promote a wedding florist, and vice versa.

- An architectural practice could work together with a landscaping contractor.

19 Build future contact into the deal for the initial sale

- Set up a short-term project team of enthusiastic marketing and salespeople to recommend ways of ensuring that even one-off sales will result in the customer needing to make a return visit. For example:
  - A car dealership could invite customers back in the month of December to collect a free calendar and pen.
  - A bookstore might give customers an invitation to a 'closed shop' evening with a guest author and where sale prices will be offered on stock items two days before being advertised to the general public.
  - An equipment installer could offer to revisit the customer after six weeks, to do a clean of the system.
- Make certain that each of these is an occasion where the customer can see something of value in the second contact.

20 Ask your salespeople and technical support staff what your products and services are worth

- Have the pricing team collect anecdotal and hard evidence about your prices, your value and what comparisons customers are making with competitive (and comparable) products or services.
  - Take care to investigate anything that is hearsay, before blindly choosing actions to take.

21 Have a very top-of-the-range option that is significantly more expensive than any other option

- Set up a short-term project team to look at your currently most expensive option for customers and identify a higher-level offer that is at least 50 per cent more expensive. Remember that the purpose of this is not necessarily to sell this option but to change their perception of value of the other options. They could consider:

- Increase speed of delivery by working 24 hours, weekends, etc.

- Significant additional after-sales care; ie weekly checks for the first month after installation and monthly for another five months.

- Add a service if you know that some customers become time-pressed; eg organize professional photos of a completed job that a client might use in brochures or on their website.

22 Ask customers for their permission to increase prices

- Personally visit 10 of your long-term customers, and have an informal discussion with them about an impending price increase. Develop your script, and test it on a C-grade customer first. For example:

  - *My accountant has been looking at our figures and the increases in our costs, etc, and we have been absorbing increases a few too many times, as you have probably seen or guessed. We are looking at a 10 per cent increase across the board, and I just wanted to make sure that I told you this face-to-face.*

- You can anticipate one of three responses:

  - Most will ask if they can meet you halfway at 5 per cent.

  - A lesser number will agree, because they do appreciate the value you add even with this increase.

  - A few will grumble aggressively, and with reluctance, and to them you could offer to defer the start date for, say, a three-month period, or perhaps agree to withhold the increase if they improve their payment periods.

  - To any C-grade customers or below that choose to walk, let them go.

23 *Develop a value strategy for any price disagreements*

- Expect price disagreements, and don't let your salespeople take the easy option of dropping the price. Instead, train them to steer the issue away from price and towards *value*.

    = Be certain that your salespeople know exactly what the value is with each product and service being offered and that they understand where this value sits relative to that being offered by competitors.

    - If they don't get the sale, you lose.

    - If they discount the price, you lose.

    - If they stick with the price, confident in its value, and offer some bonus items to secure the sale, then you have the greatest opportunity to impress and retain the customer, and in most instances the customer will be delighted to have received some bonuses. Examples include free delivery, assistance with installation, a longer warranty period, an offer of discounts on future spare parts (should they become needed).

- Ask the pricing team to develop a set of value-added options, listed in order starting with things that have the least impact on your profit. The sales team must then be trained to be smart when selecting additional items to secure the sale.

24 *Revise your price list, to show value features first*

- Pricing is only one factor in your customers' buying decisions, so it is in your interest to create a focus on non-pricing things; that is, show the value:

    - Convenience of your location for pre-purchase meetings, after-sales support, delivery of spares.

    - Quality of your products and services.

    - Technical capability of your people.

    - Reputation of your company; for example, a strong background of developing new products and owning patents; lists of awards gained.

- Whole-of-life costs; that is, purchase price *plus* longevity of the product.

- Special features, highlighting those that your competitors cannot possibly offer.

- Anything else that shows your products and services represent better value than those offered by the competition.

25 Set up payment options that ease the impact of a high price

- Establish payment methods that allow your customers to choose your highest-profit products and services, while being able to select an easy payment method. The method does impact enormously on customers' perception of price.

  - The easiest method is to allow payments over, say, 36 months. But this does add a collection risk.

  - The next is credit card, which delays the customer's actual payment by four to six weeks. It could be four weeks before the customer sees the impact of the high price.

  - A debit card means that the transaction appears on a statement at a later date, possibly six months away. The entering of a PIN means that the high purchase price itself isn't front-of-mind to the customer at the time of purchase.

- Take into consideration specific demographic issues in your client base. Pensioners, students, high earners and different socio-economic groups each approach any purchase with a certain set of attitudes to price. Design ways for your salespeople to offer payment methods appropriate for each group.

26 Start out with a simple approach

- Here are some guidelines to ensure that you actually *do stuff* without getting bogged down doing *stuff all*. Constraints will be especially important if you create a pricing team, because they will otherwise become overwhelmed right at the start.

- When thinking about your products, services and bundling-up deals, stick to a Gold, Silver and Bronze hierarchy of offers. Platinum can be added later.

- When thinking about your customers, group them into A-grade, B-grade and C-grade hierarchy based on the total profit they generate for your business. Pricing strategies must focus on the A-grade clients, never on the C-grades.

- Test out new strategies in one branch, as a pilot. This is manageable, and then replication across other branches becomes easy.

- When doing mathematical analysis, focus on a small sample that has wide impact. This might mean choosing the top 10 customers (rather than 200) or selecting the biggest selling 20 products/services (rather than 500). Such data is usually quick to obtain, and any inaccuracy in the figures has low impact on decisions. Successful strategies can then be cascaded down to the smaller clients and the lesser products/services.

- This point needs to be repeated. Watch carefully what the Team does (or appoint an external facilitator) so that they do stay focussed. Their first recommendations to you need to happen within four weeks of the start date, with profit impact being measured and reported within eight weeks.

27 Add services to your products

- Set up a three-person short-term project team with two long-term salespeople and one out-of-the-box thinker. Ask them to prepare a long list of services that can complement your products and which aim to extend the relationships with customers. Their recommendations should also include an analysis of profit impact, so that the list is presented in order. Examples:

  - Selling a lawnmower with the offer of a basic maintenance tutorial six months later plus an advanced tutorial at the 12-month mark. *Value £75, but for you £10.*

– Offering a two-for-one card for the purchase of replacement blades, spark plugs and air filters.

28 Productize your services

- Set up a three-person short-term project team with two long-term salespeople and one out-of-the-box thinker. Ask them to prepare a long list of products that can complement your services and which aim to extend the relationships with customers. Their recommendations should also include an analysis of profit impact, so that the list is presented in order. Examples:

  – A builder could offer two ongoing service packages for the slowest months: *December / Christmas Check-up* – correct sticking doors and windows, clean glass windows inside and out, wash light fittings, replace high-up light bulbs, lubricate all door hinges, polish brassware. Or a *January Repairs* – replace tap washers, touch-up furniture and timberwork scratches, fix cracked tiles, re-grout, replace broken window panes.

  – A law firm could offer a newly-weds package of services, bundling up wills, home rental agreement checking, future mortgage transaction work, life insurance for the couple, and other products. In this example, the law firm would present a small booklet of vouchers in a bright colour, because the services may be used several years in the future.

29 Uncertainty and vagueness lead to 'no sale'

- Find a person who is skilled at communication and have them 'shadow' some of your salespeople (and include telesales operators). Their role is to collect examples of vagueness when your salespeople are engaging their customers. Examples:

  – *I don't know what the delivery fee will be, so I will have to check and let you know. – That combination will be somewhere between £3,000 to £5,000. It depends.*

   – *I know it is very fragile, but on some occasions I think we
      have included additional insurance cover or it might have
      been the customer who organized that.*

   – *That colour is available, but whether our supplier has stocks
      in the country is another matter.*

● Then set up a short-term team to write mini training modules
   for your salespeople. They are to transpose all the examples
   into their counterparts, which are solid and offer certainty to
   the customer; ie *There is normally a delivery fee, but I will
   check now and see what I can do for you.* The training must
   be rolled out to every salesperson.

● As a secondary exercise, assign a detail-conscious person (not
   necessarily in sales) to review every printed brochure, your
   web pages and standard sales presentations. This task requires
   looking at those through the eyes of a customer, and
   highlighting anything that appears vague or open to
   interpretation. What they uncover then needs correction,
   probably by a different person.

30 Quotes are won on diligence not price

*Note: this Action is not about pricing; however, it impacts directly on
your volume of work and hence your profitability. If possible, have
a finance person measure the impact on your bottom line.*

● Hold a workshop with the people in your business who issue
   quotes. Have one person bring a huge hand-drawn flowchart
   of the quotation process.

● Step through the process, and identify every box where control
   is handed off to the customer (and by inference your own
   people are detached).

● Now insert a control step immediately after those boxes,
   requiring a salesperson to keep front-of-mind with the
   customer; ie *Chase quote after three days.*

● To complete this, ensure that Standard Operating Procedures
   and training modules are updated to reflect the adjusted
   process and the responsibilities of key people are defined.

31 There is only one way to grow your business rapidly and for least effort

- Through your own personal behaviour, build a pricing culture by always asking focussed questions. The most common scenario is when your sales and marketing manager presents you with a proposal to do one of these 'standard' things:
  - A project to win more customers.
  - A project to prevent the loss of customers.
  - A project to increase the frequency of interactions between your business and each customer.
  - A project to reduce costs or increase productivity.
  - A project to purchase technology items for the sales force.

- Your standard response must always be, *Please go away and run an analysis with our finance people showing the profit impact of simply raising the prices by 5 per cent. Do the same for your proposed project, and I will approve the one with the higher impact.*

32 Don't let one bad experience colour your judgement

- Find a person who is skilled at communication and have them conduct interviews with every salesperson, gathering stories of their best and worst experience(s) and inquiring about the effect of that on their confidence.

- Write these up as mini case studies, in this format:
  - *Situation*: what happened.
  - *Effect*: how the salesperson felt, and how long that feeling impacted on their confidence.
  - *The If-Only Alternative*: a better way that this could have been handled so that the salesperson's confidence was repaired rapidly.

- Ensure that the scale of these experiences is placed in context with their whole experience; ie how many bad experiences from how many sales calls.

33 Re-direct the 'Let's please the customer' culture

- To take this Action, you need to be very clear, so that the ambiguity is not lost. The tragedy of 'Please the customer' is the *implied* '...no matter what'. Your version needs to be 'Please the customer by offering value aligned with price'. So, your salespeople need to see discounting as the very final resort, after value offerings are exhausted.

- Have a training person write this into any appropriate training modules, and wherever possible include role-play exercises.

- Change your discounting procedures such that the offering of a discount can never be done on the spot, in the presence of a customer. Building in a 24-hour delay of approval will go a long way towards keeping salespeople confined to using value alternatives, which are better for the customer anyway.

34 Offering certainty is creating higher value, for higher price

- Ask the pricing team to investigate areas where customers feel uncertainty, and recommend methods to build in certainty at a price. The best domestic example of this is extended warranty on white goods. Consumers can buy coverage for years three to five on the purchase of major electrical items.

- This could include a *change of mind* and money-back guarantee, or *if you see it at a lower price we will refund the difference*, etc.

35 Repeat customers are much more valuable than one-time sales

- Whatever business you are in, design methods which will ensure that repeat customers are identified when they return. Delegate this to a short-term team of salespeople, with possible input from an IT specialist. Examples of this that work:

  - Human memory: a top New York barperson can recall 3,000 people's names and their drinks.

  - Computer systems: the smartphone system 'Vend' alerts sales staff in retail outlets when the customer walks through the front door. The POS screens show their face avatar and a list of key words.

  - Loyalty clubs: frequent buyer programmes can operate internationally and require the member to pay an annual fee, or in the simplest form it could be a piece of cardboard that identifies a returning café patron.

- Design into your sales and marketing roll-out programmes that every special offer is presented to existing customers ahead of new customers.

36 Get an external perspective

- Identify 15 business owners who are in different industries to you and not competitors of yours. Using referees, reduce this to eight who are the most business-savvy and whose companies have been operating profitably for at least five years. Invite them to a one-day workshop to discuss pricing strategies for mutual benefit.

- Ask the people to contribute to this Agenda:

  a Welcome and Statement of Purpose (to develop better pricing strategies) – you (10 min).

  b Introductions (business overview, major products or services, summary of typical customers) – each participant (5 min each).

c Presentations of approach to the setting of prices and summary of pricing strategy – each participant (30 min each).

d Produce a joint pricing strategy capturing the best points from each business.

e Group dinner.

Notes: 1) consider utilizing an independent facilitator; 2) if you see benefit, the group may agree to doing a similar workshop regularly, on a different topic.

37 Adopt and adapt from your competitors

- Look around your competitors, ask your customers and ask everyone you meet, 'What is one thing that XYZ does really well?' Listen with an open mind and see whether you can use these ideas yourself. Tip: copying your competitors just makes you their equal – always go one better.

38 Eliminate cost plus pricing from your strategies

- Delegate this to the pricing team, and eliminate cost plus within six weeks.

39 Focus your salespeople on value, not cost

- Have a business-savvy senior salesperson remove all references to cost from resources that salespeople can access. Also include a review of training modules.

- Then have them work with a training professional to develop new training materials that have a focus on value. The culture you want to create is one in which salespeople will sell 'up to' the value, not sell 'down' to the cost.

- Finally, have the sales managers train their own sales team in these modules.

40 Any sale is a compromise of issues

- Refer back to the triangle in Chapter 5 and have a training professional design this into your sales approach.
- Train the salespeople to use this tool.

41 Value dissipates with time

- For the products and services where you have gone above and beyond to create value for the customer, send your invoices at the time when the customer most appreciates the value. For a professional services firm, this is invariably on the day that the job is completed.
- Adjust your accounting system appropriately so that this happens.

42 Always offer a 'one-up' option

- Presenting customers with a single option is tantamount to saying take-it-or-leave-it, and leaving it is not what you want. As the customer is considering a single option, have your salesperson present a 'one-up' alternative. In some cases, the customer will take that option, but more likely they will make the original purchase, simply because they can see it is cheaper *relative* to the one-up.
- In addition, have the pricing team group your most popular or most profitable products or services into 'classes'. For example:
  - Gold, Silver, Bronze
  - Large, Medium, Small
  - Bulk, Regular, Light
  - Luxury, Regular, Budget

Two questions, with answers

Where do you start? As a guide, what pace is reasonable?

1 Today: Get ready to implement the 5 per cent price increase across the board. Call your senior people together tomorrow morning.

2 Tomorrow: Make the announcement without inviting debate, then discuss and agree on the effective date. Customers will need to be notified, so the first of the next month should be your target.

3 The day after: Choose any 14 Actions from the 42 suggestions above. Create a Project Plan to implement these over the following six months.

4 The following half-year: Choose another 14, and implement.

5 The next half-year: Implement the remaining 14.

6 When you have attacked all 42, start again and push the boundaries further.

THIS STUFF WORKS!

16 The final word on pricing for profit

There are many ways in which a business can aim to improve its profits. Most will follow the traditional routes of simply seeking to grow top line turnover, or a programme of action to reduce their costs, but the truth is that the easiest and the quickest route to increase the bottom line of any business is to get your pricing right.

Ultimately, the decision to adopt and adapt the ideas in this book is yours. Although some areas of the topic have a level of complexity that requires you to do some research and preparation, at its heart it really is very simple. You just have to make a choice to charge more.

It is, however, important to understand that in doing this you may end up treading on many toes as you seek to challenge some of the entrenched ideas within your business or of your colleagues. Argument and debate is no bad thing as it helps to develop balanced and reasoned approaches for any proposed changes. However, it is imperative that this debate is open and based on facts and evidence, not anecdotes and hearsay. If someone at the sharp end of your business resists an idea you want to implement, ask them to explain and evidence their point of view rather than just use it as an excuse to avoid change.

There are countless businesses that have used the ideas and concepts covered in the book, some of whom would not still be in business today had they not done so, and many others that have made enormous improvements to their profits and hence financial stability and future prosperity.

The very early chapters explained the background maths of the issue, ie that the impact of small changes in pricing has a much more dramatic impact than similarly small changes in winning customers, or selling extras or any other strategy to grow profits that you might choose.

The logic of the book boils down to a very simple premise:

1 Increasing prices will increase the turnover and hence the profitability of the business.

2 Increasing prices *may* cause some customers to stop buying.

The only decision for any business seeking to improve its profit is whether the benefit of 1) is greater than the consequence of 2).

In this book I therefore concentrated on two key aspects. The first was to give you the confidence that in the vast majority of businesses the impact of 1) is significantly greater than the possible downside of 2). In fact, in many examples the impact of 2) was quite simply nothing at all, and in only the most extreme situations does it out-weigh the upside of the extra turnover and profit.

The second aspect was to give you techniques and ideas on how you can achieve a price increase without it necessarily being seen that way by your customers. More sophisticated presentation, better packaging and bundling of products and services all help to focus your customers' attention on the value you deliver rather than the price that you charge. A sharper eye on discounts given away, or on which customers you really make money from, will help to keep you focussed on where profits are made and where they are given away.

Having read the book, it is now a choice for you as to whether you work through each of the individual chapter Action Points, picking out the issues that you intend to work on, analysing and planning a controlled project for gradual improvements, or whether you go back to Chapter 15 and just take each idea and run with it as suggested. Either way, it requires you to make a decision to invest more time and effort into this business-critical subject than you do at present.

So what would I recommend you do now?

In the vast majority of projects to improve profitability that I have seen, significant time and effort has been lost in thinking too much about all of the *what if* scenarios of any proposals. There are a good number of ideas in this book that are quite simply blindingly obvious common sense, such as getting better control over discounts.

The best advice is therefore to take the two or three ideas that seem most relevant to your business, and have a go at them straight away. Do not spend too much time thinking about it and get the classic 'paralysis of analysis', just get on with something simple and do it straight away.

Perhaps the most important step is to change your approach to the pricing issue. You need to ensure that pricing is seen as simply another business skill to be learned, developed and implemented in your business, and one that needs continual attention and constant reappraisal and adjustment.

Many of the end of chapter Action Points referred to a pricing team, comprising key senior people in your team with a balance of skills, from frontline selling to understand your customers, financial analysis and accounting expertise to get a grip on the numbers, and personnel or HR skills to help embrace change and institutionalize the positive changes needed. Build people around you who get comfortable with the topic and who can build their experiences and knowledge to help drive change.

But if you want the simple answer, and don't have the time or resources to tackle the subject in such a structured way, just put your prices up. The customers or sales you lose are in all probability not making you any profit at the moment anyway, but even if they are, they will be less than the extra profit you make from the majority of happy customers who continue to value and appreciate the value you already deliver.

Good luck.

INDEX

NB: page numbers in *italic* indicate figures or tables

Also available from **Kogan Page**

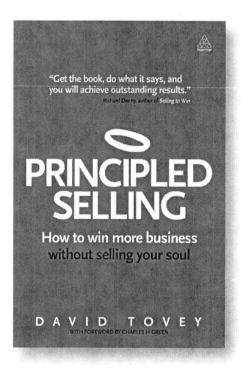

Find out more; visit **www.koganpage.com** and
sign up for offers and regular e-newsletters.

KoganPage

Also available from **Kogan Page**

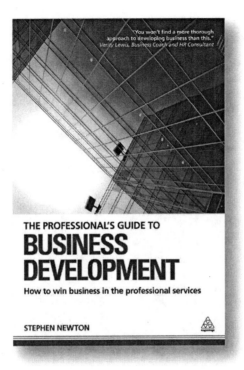

Find out more; visit **www.koganpage.com** and
sign up for offers and regular e-newsletters.

Also available from **Kogan Page**

Find out more; visit **www.koganpage.com** and
sign up for offers and regular e-newsletters.

With over 1,000 titles in printed and digital format, **Kogan Page** offers affordable, sound business advice

www.koganpage.com

KoganPage

CPSIA information can be obtained at www.ICGtesting.com
Printed in the USA
LVOW08s1207160713

343124LV00005B/116/P